# DON'T LET MY TEARS FOOL YOU

## THE WAR IS ON

BY DASHAUN "JIWE" MORRIS

Printed in the United States of America

First Printing, 2015

ISBN- 13: 978-0692506004

ISBN- 10: 0692506004

5iveDentertainment

P.O. box 455

LoveJoy, GA 30250

Cover design: Rodney Clancy www.rclancy.dunked.com

Photographs: @ShannonMcCollum

Edited: Liza Chowdhury

Creative writer: Bob Dixon

*For information regarding special discounts for bulk purchases, please contact me at Dontletmytearsfoolyou@gmail.com

**From the Author of**

**“War of the Bloods In My Veins”**

**And Filmmaker of**

**"Deathcoast Str8 Outta Newark"**

**Recipient of 2008 African American Literary Award for Best Memoir**

**Nominated for the 41st NAACP Image Award for Best Memoir**

*This book is dedicated to Andrea. Your love is Paramount. You are such a beautiful woman. I love you mama.*

# Foreword

My mother was just a young woman in her 20's when she witnessed the assassination of her husband, Malcolm X Shabazz. One week prior on Valentine's Day, a Molotov cocktail was thrown into the nursery of her home where my sisters and I slept as babies. When my father was killed, my mother was left traumatized, frightened and alone. She was a young woman with four babies and pregnant with twins. My mother had six daughters. I often asked myself how was she able to overcome so many obstacles. She never accepted "no" or "I can't" as an answer for herself. She raised six girls proud to be women, proud to be of the African Diaspora, and proud to be Muslims. She raised us knowing that we are our brother and sisters' keeper.

I believe that every child should have an opportunity to feel good about themselves. A child should feel safe and secure simply "to be". I believe that no matter where we find ourselves in the world, the opportunities to be all of whom we can be, should be limitless. However, I read a poll conducted on adolescents who were asked, "What would you like to be when you grow up?" The answer was "RICH". They did not want to be rich in service or rich in helping anyone, but just RICH... and it touched me. What happened? To focus on material gain ONLY should be unacceptable when you know that you are worth far more than that.

It breaks my heart to see any child without love, protection and guidance; without ambition and vision; without compassion and a sense of humanity. I believe that every child must be nurtured to feel good about him/herself. You must be inspired and to know you are worthy of a quality education so that you recognize your value to participate in the mainstream of society—and give something back to our community; to love others almost as much as you love yourselves; to have care and compassion for others almost as much as you have for yourselves and to desire to give something back to society as much as you desire to give to yourselves.

Each one of us has the power to co-exist peacefully, to be **effective, dynamic leaders**—and to actually be the change that is needed in today's society, to change this nation and to create that legacy of your own. Nelson Mandela said, "When a man has done what he considers to be his duty for his people and his country, he can then rest in peace." BUT only YOU can make the decision to assume your leadership roles in your homes as well as your communities.

Some of our young people are living in a world where society dictates whom they will be, placing man-made obstacles in their paths, making their challenges more difficult when 60% of Black & Latino young men are shackled within the confines of jails and prisons throughout this country. Babies are giving birth to babies without a clue as to what it takes to raise a healthy child with a "properly" formed identity intact. Fathers are sometimes gone, leaving mothers to be both parents; children disrespecting elders, disrespecting one another and not respecting themselves. They are killing one another over turfs when the land isn't owned by any of us. And so you must ask yourselves, what exactly am I fighting for? What does my life represent? What is my legacy?

I am proud to call Jiwe, my friend, because he remains committed to sharing his journey, his trials and tribulations with you in hopes of shedding light… to help not only his Blood brothers and sisters but all young people claim a life that is worthy to themselves as well as in the eyes of God. He understands the importance of self-respect and respect for others; the absolute importance of compassion and truth and the importance of leadership in order to produce the best in your selves that mankind can offer. I invite you to take this journey into Jiwe's inner most thoughts as he comes to terms with his true Manhood. He allows us to see the desperation of a young man who once was engulfed in gang life as a means of survival and the turmoil he faces.

- Ilyasah Shabazz

# Prologue

"Who dat nigga think he is!"

They angry at me, I thought about it, meditated, really thought hard about the WHY? I kept hearing of conversations people were having about me because of my new outlook in life.

Look at dat nigga ova there succeeding. Who he think he is being happy. Oh so he think he deserve to have a family, a house, off probation, no more charges? That nigga ain't shit! Fuck his book I ain't reading shit. Real gangsters don't read. Look at us, long as I can count this fetty we making I'm Gucci. We still out here and we stayed down for the set. We ain't never left and never gonna' leave. That nigga sold out. Fuck his movies, I can make a better one. That nigga found God, foh, that nigga a sucker. We the real ones. The streets love us, we are the streets, that nigga whack, I'll push dat nigga onna set! Feel me, who he think he is?

Gonna' move his family to a better environment? Foh, onna set this shit for life. Who he think he is? Being happy now, nigga I ain't happy, so fuck his happiness, fuck his family, fuck his success, fuck his life. How that nigga keep beating all his cases? Matter fact that nigga snitching! Word yea, let niggas know he telling. Ain't no God saving nobody all them times. My nigga Lil' Killer doin' 50 years for some shit he did 1 time. This nigga had 3 attempted murder cases and beat them all? Foh, he telling. He ain't real no more, he sold out. Real niggas never leave. My big homee said we gon' die for the set, yup yup that's right, ima die for my homees. I love my hood, my niggas love me back.

Fuck a job. I ain't working fo' no white man. nigga I make like $200 a day out here in da trap. Niggas respect us that's what it's about. This nigga on some spiritual shit now, foh real niggas stay in da shit. Anyways, I'm tired of talking about this nigga, yea me too, that's all we do. Aight so homee what u bout to do? Shit, probably smoke, dump a oxy, fuck a bitch and probably talk shit about this nigga some more tomorrow. What you bout to do? Shit, nuffin', probably da same. Hell, we both ain't doing shit, but I tell u what, we both ain't never supporting that nigga.

The response coming soon!

Just turn the page.......

Damn! It amazes me when I think back to all them nights drinking and drugging, banging and ganging. Now knowing that the very people I would die for are the very people that despise me. Well let's not give them too much credit, it's unwarranted. But I will tell these two, eye to eye! "Are u serious!?" You mean to tell me after all I sacrificed in these bloody streets, all the pain and stress over the years, you have the balls to fix yo' mouth to me that way?! See part of the problem is all them drugs still up in you. You think I owe you something? See the difference between you two and me is that y'all still believe the crap these streets teaching you. I finally realized what they taught me was all a lie. It took me 24 years of losing friends, my freedom, family and my sanity to realize it was all lies. The code y'all pushing on me to be loyal to, I don't and won't live by anymore.

I've had enough dark days in my life to understand this light that's on me now. I deserve and actually like it. Yea, I've made a lot of mistakes in the streets but I also did a lot right. My change only makes you uncomfortable because deep down, I believe you want some for yourself, but you so SUNK in SIN, DRUGS, PILLS, LIQUOR, RANDOM COOCH, so far in the field that you don't even know how to fathom the IDEA let alone possibility of it and your pissed at me because I figured it out. Well check this out homee, I can show you and teach you the steps I took. Each of our journeys are different and everything that works for me probably won't work for you, but damn it it's a starting point. If you think yo' words or slander will force me to act like a nigga again well newsflash, it wont! I wasn't duck sauce back then, still ain't now, but what I am now is more tolerable. I can endure a lot of the mess y'all dishin'. Deep down I still be pissed, I still want heads to roll, but I've learned the art of channeling, balancing out the crave, the anger, and not risking my freedom. Not only that, a fool just tired of hurting people. I been doing that since I was 11. Maybe all this change stuff is too much for you to comprehend, hell, I'm still figuring it out, but one thing for sure, I like my life much better on this side.

Where you are I can never return and as much as this will make you uncomfortable, I hope and pray you crossover one day. Every night when my head touch that floor, I speak life into you. I pray over your soul. Not necessarily that good things come to you because I'd be a freakin' liar, but I do pray that the God I run with now, do for you what HE did for me. I mean that. You wanna' kill me yo'? Well that also is something you have no control over because what is will be. I ain't trippin' 'bout that though. I've taught my babies enough to last them a life time. I've planted a lot of seeds around this country that I pray people will continue to water, and I've repented for every little act of violence, crime that I could remember. Just remember this, as I now have to slide, in the event of a tragedy, crisis or hardship, even at this point with all that's goin on, the rumors, the slander, all of it, I'd still be there for you if yo' issue came my way, as a brother, probably sooner than the guys you claim you will still die for. So I leave you with this last thought, and never ever ever.....ever forget these words that's about to leave my mouth. You probably like nigga you crazy, why the hell would you do anything for me knowing how I feel about you.

(At this point I would definitely get up on ‘em close because they need to see my pupils.)

Then this should be the only PROOF! that you need to know GOD is real because if I acted in my FLESH, this conversation wouldn't have gotten this far, jus the BIG 3, my shell hittin’ the ground, followed by yo’ body and then my exit! BOOOOOOOM! Don’t play with my God. That man delivered me from a sickness. I ride fo’ HIM the looooong way! You should too!

# CHAPTER 1

For most of my life I was surrounded by cold concrete sidewalks that were adorned with chalked body figures. I became accustomed to the cautionary yellow tape that highlighted the frequent appearances of crime scenes. Exposed to the rough inner city streets of Newark, NJ, I encountered endless acts of violence which primarily stemmed from what appeared to be inescapable self-hatred from minds that were unable to navigate a way out. Many were misguided just like I and they soothed the horrors of "street life" through drug dependency and criminal activity.

As a child, I was abandoned by my father while mama struggled with her addiction so I was forced to survive on my own. The lack of unconditional love and parental guidance forced me into independence at an early age. As an abandoned child, I looked to "street life" for protection and power. I always had a yearning and desire to be something great, but I was limited because I was confined to my hood and in the midst of learning how to survive, I was crowned a gangster. Love was replaced by survival and this in turn created the animal I was for several years. It took me 20 years to finally realize that "street dreams" would ultimately turn into nightmares that would forever haunt me and to this day the scars and wounds remain unhealed. In my 30 plus years of living, I have lost so much to the streets, but by the grace of God, I have survived. As a survivor, I always had a desire to provide others with opportunities to live a better life as well.

I shared my life story through my memoir, "War of the Bloods in my Veins." Since the release of the book in 2008, I have lived my life openly by agreeing to be a part of documentaries and films that shed light on the realities of gang life, being fatherless and inner city violence. I am what you would refer to as a "ghetto/hood celebrity." Despite all of the violent encounters of my past, the obstacles I have lived through have helped me to create a platform that has inspired several others both nationally and internationally. I wrote as a means of survival while I was in prison. The walls stifled me and writing allowed me to escape the mental instability that overwhelms you in the confines of a cell. The words that expressed the pain and sorrow of my youth helped to create many opportunities for me upon my release from prison and I was able to do a total 180 from the life I once lived.

My first book had been released by Simon and Schuster in 2008. I had let so many people down when I went to prison because I once had the opportunity to become scouted as a professional football player. Although I missed my opportunity at the NFL and am still somewhat bitter about it, I took a long look in the mirror and felt good about where my life was headed today. I escaped going to prison for 25 years and was now a successful published author. I remember the feeling I felt walking into Barnes and Nobles and seeing my book on the shelf. I felt as if time had stopped and the moment had stolen my breath because I was speechless and astonished by the idea that my life was worthy enough to be used as a literary tool to inspire others. My book had made an impact that no touchdown I ever could have scored on a Sunday could make. This moment was overwhelmed with the feeling of pride and accomplishment.

I remember promising my mother at the age of 16 that I would buy her a house and get her out of the ghetto. Every little boy who lives in the hood has a dream of getting his family out of the turmoil and chaos of the old neighborhood. I was no different. The cash advance from my book allowed me to finally make this dream of mine come true. Newark helped make me who I am, but the rowdiness, the liveliness and abundance of prospects to potentially make another bad decision made it imperative for me to leave and start a new beginning. I moved my family to a cul-de-sac in Atlanta, Georgia. In my mind, I had made it. My mother, wife and children were out of the disorder of inner city life and I felt like I was released from the suffocation of New Jersey. My first night in the suburbs of Georgia, I remember feeling so free and walking at 2 a.m. looking at the sky and even the stars seemed different. I felt at peace. Moving to Atlanta was a symbol of a new beginning for me and my family.

When I reflect back on my life in comparison to where I am today; I see exactly how I have uncomfortably become a "fish out of water." I have maintained a close knit bond with men that I grew up with in the same neighborhood streets. With every step of perseverance, I found ways to involve them, gifting them opportunities most men from the inner city never see and I freely shared my successes on numerous occasions. As I climbed the ladders of success; it was essential for me to lift up my homees as well so that those behind me could have a way out too. I have even sacrificed a few opportunities because of those very same guys. So when I think of myself as a "fish out of water," I want to paint a true picture of who I was and who I have blossomed into today because based on statistics, a hardcore street gangster was never supposed to make it this far. Here I am a GANGBANGER, someone who has lived a lifestyle that America stigmatizes and I am now forced into a position in which I must inspire others even though I myself have yet to be healed. I have to walk the thin line of success and at the same time show loyalty to the streets I had pledged my life to for so long. No one gave me a book of directions on how to balance and maneuver this new life I was blessed with, but I tried my best to make everyone happy even if it meant forgetting about myself in the midst of it.

# CHAPTER 2

Balancing this new success, being loyal to the streets and being a family man is no easy task. Growing up, I never knew what marriage looked like. I married Neina because she is the epitome of an all American wife. By giving me my four children, she gave my life a new meaning. For as long as I can remember, Neina has always been my back bone. I met her when I was struggling because I had been kicked out of college after my all American year. The beginnings of our relationship were overshadowed by my struggles of trying to get back into school. I went through hell getting back on campus for violating the no weapons on campus rule. When she met me, I was ready to give up and tired from all of the conflicts with school. However, she always found a way to lift my spirits and stay by my side. Her unwavering support and love helped me to connect with her in a way I never connected with any other person. Neina is my safe haven. I was forced to be this tough and bad person in the streets, but I was able to let my guard down and feel comfort and safety in Neina's arms at night. She is my rock.

As the years passed, I took her through hell in our relationship. I introduced her to a world that she hadn't known. But she loved me through it all. Neina loved Dashaun, but hated my public image of Jiwe. It is funny that I was born with the name Dashaun, but I never got to know who Dashaun was because he stopped maturing at the age of nine when he first was introduced to the street life. Now Jiwe, that is the name my god father T Rodgers gave me. Much of my identity and fame is tied to the name Jiwe. I never thought that Neina would have a problem with me gaining success; I mean what woman wouldn't want a handsome, smart and successful man?

The fame came with a cost and jeopardized our relationship. She had to compete with the many women I had available to me. My new world had an abundance of models, strippers, successful, and even married women. I completely lost my damn mind. I always had the attention of girls growing up because I was a quiet loner and this intrigued them, but since 2008, the type of women I attracted was the baddest of the bad. I really didn't think I was a bad guy. In my mind, I thought this came with fame. My reasoning was that as long as I took care of home, didn't bring no disease back, and not have no women calling me and getting outta' pocket, I could juggle both marriage and the outside affairs. I was riding high, traveling to hotels, night clubs and getting attention at all of these V.I.P. events. All I heard was Jiwe this and Jiwe that. It was always Jiwe...Jiwe...Jiwe. I got used to my name being mentioned often, my presence being needed, wanted, desired, feared, respected, and being admired.

So many new things were occurring and I did not have an opportunity to adjust and prioritize my life. Let's be real, how in the hell do you go from being a gang banging, college expelled, animal to participating in speaking events at Susan Taylor's house. I now had to get used to riding in limos with Terry McMillan and engaging in panels side by side with former Ambassador Edward Perkins? I mean how many people with my background have an opportunity to become involved in these types of events? So you can imagine how surreal things were to me.

After all of this attention, coming home would be a blow to my ego because I was no longer this big deal anymore. In my house, Jiwe didn't exist, I was just Daddy. This always bothered me about Neina. When I got national notoriety, she never made me feel like I was that big of a name, perhaps because she didn't like what I was becoming. Once I stepped outside of the house, lights camera action and Jiwe is in full fucking effect. I never considered Neina's emotions and how she felt about my constant traveling, late night phone calls and me constantly being needed by others. I just assumed that as a wife she was supposed to stay home and take care of my kids and let me go out and do what I'm supposed to do. In the meantime, I would be out in the streets caught up in the life of Jiwe and would not check in with my wife.

Chasing fame and trying to be a family man at the same time are very difficult. My world became consumed by chasing money. Traveling and networking became my priority and my greed for fame and fortune began getting in the way of caring for my wife and children. These are the unseen struggles that never get publicized when you see people getting famous and making it out of nowhere to becoming a person that is instantly recognized. I think about all the kids from the hood that have athletic talent and get snatched up by big time colleges to play a sport and then end up going pro and people wonder why they end up doing stupid stuff such as getting arrested, what the hell did you think was going to happen? This is the same thing they have been doing since they were eight, now they just doing it with a spotlight on them and they have absolutely no idea how to handle the situation.

Everybody at some point in their lives needs positive guidance, inspiration from people who not only understand the struggles that they are facing, but someone who can also show them how to properly cope with these new pressures. Fame and fortune are things that are sold by the American media as cure all's but that simply ain't the truth. Without proper guidance and humility, fame and fortune are a loaded weapon in the hands of a person without a strong moral foundation, sooner or later it's going to go off and someone is going to get hurt. I learned these lessons the hard way and as a consequence, hurt the closest person to me which is Neina.

Many people think Neina Morris is a lucky woman. I don't see it that way. If people knew the damage I caused over 10 years I am sure you would think differently. Most people get to see one element of my being because of the person I am supposed to be in the public eye. Neina was there during the time I wasn't this way, I think I'm the lucky one because she stayed with me all of these years and put up with all my shit which includes jail, prison, depression, episodes in my sleep, mood swings, homees living in our house, always puttin' da hood before her, exposing her to my violent ways in the streets & so much more. Despite all of the pain, she continues to be a supportive wife and inspiring mother.

In addition to marriage, fatherhood was also something I never thought I would be good at. After all, I was living the life of a gangster, on a destructive path, which usually leads to death. How could I care for a child? People ask me where my anger comes from and why am I so upset. I think it is mostly because of the void I feel due to the part of me I don't know. As a young boy, I did not meet him and was looking for a face to match my own. There were no tools handed to a prince by his KING. Imagine that, 18 years walking in my own shadow, angry, swinging bats, just lost out here. I had no guidance, love or none of that. I was trying to find an older face like mine, bigger hands like these, a taller man with a deeper voice that looks just like me. I ended up standing eye to eye with my dad eventually.

My mom ran into my half-sister who had a number for me. I dialed the number with hopes that I would not get through and could avoid the situation. When he did answer, I remember saying to myself "Damn Dae, he sounds just like you." My mom never spoke about him, never told me shit. Here I am 18 years old, setting up a meeting to have a face to face conversation with him. Later I'm in his living room for a short, awkward visit. There were so many things I wanted to say but I couldn't find the words to express all I had bottled inside of me. I just knew I wanted a friendship with him to get past all of the hurt. I wanted to leave with a better sense of myself because I felt that there was still so much left to know about my history. My hopes were that maybe we will create a bond as time progresses and we will eventually grow to have a better relationship.

Later my eyes would fill with steam and my fists would tighten as my mother shared her experiences with my father. My mom shared her pain. It was a hard pill to swallow. How could he beat her, mistreat her, leave her with open wounds and blood. I couldn't take the pain, a second bloody visit was all I could envision. All of my anger, coupled with my mother's pain was enough to beat his ass. After all, I was the son of the streets. He may have not been there for me, but the number blocks and avenues raised me. I beat him lifeless and left him bloody in his living room. My half- brother pulled out his gun on me and I pulled out mine. There we were, two brothers pointing guns at each other. We looked at each other in the eye and dared to see who would shoot first, but neither one of us pulled the trigger.

So much for that bond I longed to have and filling the emptiness of the other half of me that was created by a man I never got to know. I was young, hurt, filled with anger and felt that he deserved that ass beating. The meeting led me back to the drawing board, but now with a whole lot more anger. The street life was all I knew, I didn't give a fuck about the dangers. For all that my father wasn't and everything we couldn't be, I learned so much about who I am and what it has done to me. I can't rewrite my past but my future definitely has a chance. A fatherless childhood wasn't the best, but, it made me a better man. It made me realize the kind of father I needed to become so my offspring would never have to endure the pain that haunted me for so many years.

From the day my daughter Dashana was born, two lives began, hers and mines. I did not think I could love her because I did not love myself. That all changed the day I watched her come into the world. Simultaneously, as she was born I had just been bailed out of jail on a first-degree attempted murder charge. The joy of her birth and the realization that I would not be going to prison created an opportunity for an instantaneous bond between she and I. When I first laid eyes on her, I realized there was nothing on the Earth that I loved more. All of my previous poor choices that I had made, which made my family suffer, could now be redeemed through fatherhood. She saved my life.

In 2007, one of my close friends was gunned down and killed in Paterson, NJ. When I received the phone call, I had every intention of seeking revenge. I remember running up the stairs, changing my clothes, and grabbing my pistol. However, I was stopped at the front door by my wife holding my daughter in her stretched out arms, screaming "What about her? Who's going to take care of her?" With the gun in my hand, tears in my eyes, and hate in my heart, I stood frozen because I had never experienced love and hate in the same moment. I had feelings of weakness and confusion as I looked at my baby. What was I supposed to do? For the first time in my life, I realized love was greater than hate because I dropped my gun and fell to the floor in tears.

Sometimes my daughter asks me why I love her so much. My response to her is, "I love you because I made you. I look at you as the female version of me. I see the same young athlete I once was. You possess the same leadership skills and drive. You represent to me everything I did not accomplish. Daddy made bad choices and my athletic career was cut short. Daddy did not have a foundation and because of what I did not have, I have come to know what you need. I am your biggest fan. You keep running because we are all counting on you. Make us all proud and make yourself proud. The foundations I am laying down now will get you to the destinations you are meant to achieve. When you get older, new things are going to come at you and you will encounter new temptations. Stay away from the fast stuff and stay close to home. Learn from your fathers mistakes. I am counting on you. You are my shining star." Dashana is my warrior princess. She made my heart beat.

I began training my daughter to run track and field at the age of three. Every day, we would run laps around the neighborhood track. It was clear that she had a gift for track and field. I did not want to raise my baby in the slums of Newark. I felt there was more opportunity and resources to nurture her track and field talent in Atlanta, Georgia and my assumptions were correct. She trained hard and excelled in competitive meets. I became the proudest father ever when she won the USATF Junior Olympics in the 1500m, setting a new national record. When I think about all the hours we spent together training, watching films in the early morning hours, researching statistics, and analyzing previous races, I realize that I had become extremely invested in her. I could not sleep because her next race was on my mind. I had abandoned a personal life to invest time in her health, conditioning, and mental tenacity.

It took some time to fully understand why I had become so consumed with pushing her to be the best. My dedication to her was the same way I obsessed in the film room at Delaware State University, slept in the weight room, got to practice early, and left late, all those characteristics are what led me to being the number one kick returner in the country in 2002. I had led the entire country for kickoff returns for touchdowns. After I missed the NFL Draft because of character issues, I became depressed and life had little meaning for me. I was so close to reaching my dream and I threw it all away. I live with these regrets until this day, but the sight of my daughter rounding the track with a support system I never had, resources that were not available to me, combined with her athletic ability restores my hope for success. My personal choices made me lose my opportunity to play professional football, athletic fame and success. I want my daughter to have the same opportunities and have me by her side so that I can guide her towards better choices.

To hear an entire stadium cheer for her as she broke national records is the same feeling I once felt when I was named as a Black college first team All American, Sports Network first team All American, and the Associated Press first team All American. As she wins competitions, we both win. I realize now more than ever that sometimes the universe blesses us with children not only for us to care, love, and provide for, but to breathe life back into us, especially those who need redemption. I am not only her provider and protector, but also I am also her biggest fan. My daughter is my second chance. My daughter has made the darkness in my heart diminish. She gave me a reason to wake up each morning. I can't thank my Lord enough for blessing me with such a beautiful child. My life had been full of prison sentences, violence, hate, pain and misery, but my daughter's birth helped me through some of the most difficult times of my life.

After Dashana, I was able to be the father of two more beautiful daughters Dasharie and Dashani. Each of them are the center of my universe. Fatherhood developed into a new meaning after the birth of my son little Dashaun. For much of my life, running the streets took so much precedence that I almost missed some of the days that no one should miss. The day my son was born brought my whole world into a whole new light, granted I had seen the world in a different light three times before when each of my baby girls were born and just as a father shares a special relationship with his daughters there is a unique bond that is created when a son is born. The birth of my son left me with a different kind of pride, a sense that my family name and traditions will be passed on. I had several questions running through my mind such as will he grow up and be like me? In many ways I hope so, in others not so much. Like most parents, I want better for my children than I ever had, I want them to have my good qualities and traits but none of my bad. In many aspects, I hope they take up after Neina.

Sacrifice is a principle that I tripped over, and my fall had major repercussions. The side effects of the injuries that I sustained were critical; however, when I took the time to look up the word sacrifice, one definition for the word was, a forfeiture of something highly valued, for the sake of one considered to have a greater value or claim. The second definition said, relinquishment of something, or to sell or give away at a loss. I read the different definitions for the word, and what I took away from it was, you had to give something up. It is a known fact among successful people that with any type of gain at some point a sacrifice was made to achieve their goals. Sacrifice is one of the primary principles necessary for growth. When examining all that this principle entails, I realized that it can become difficult. I guess that's the reason why I ignored it in the past because there was no room for me to have an, "I don't give a fuck attitude." As I began to hold the hand of sacrifice I asked her if she can walk with me slowly, because I am new to this like a baby and needed her to nurture me. Since the streets had a stronghold on me for so long, it is still difficult for me to not put them first. The things you give up are usually the things you really want to do, that is the part that brought agony to my spirit and heart. Unfortunately, from the age of 10, adding to the agonizing thoughts that sometimes keep me up all night I was already hard wired by the streets. I have a lot of learned behavior that I have picked up over the years that became second nature to me. The transitions were initially difficult because I had to retrain myself or rewire myself. That's the part that will make you short circuit at times because it requires discipline and for several years my discipline was focused on negative activities. This all took patience which I had very little of. I remember walking in baby stages of sacrifice and I was reminiscing over some of the activities that I was involved in on the streets, and how I put myself in some situations where I was sacrificing my life.

Now that I have a better understanding of the word, the question that I would ask myself is, "what was the purpose of my sacrifice?" Then, I began asking myself other questions and I didn't like the answers that I was coming up with. Then, I realized that ever since I can remember I have been making sacrifices. The path that I'm walking on today, I'm aware of the ones that I want to make and will benefit from them. I was suddenly locked down as I was holding sacrifice's hand and to my surprise she slipped the cuffs on me, and on the other hand she cuffed my family to me.

I locked myself into my responsibilities that I had in the home, and it also cut my possibilities of encountering danger because at any time when I'm in the streets it can go down. It was the beginning of a new transformation for me. I had to adapt quickly because I was the only caretaker for my daughter while my wife was at work. I didn't have a playbook on being a father I was a full time gangster dedicated to the streets. Now, my reality has changed I'm no longer locked down in any jail cell, I'm locked down in the house all day with my daughter. I quickly began to recognize and become familiar with a side of me that I never experienced before. Prior to becoming a father, I was just a hard motherfucker all the time. With fatherhood, I had to learn something new and it is unfamiliar to my lifestyle. My mentality, actions, and habits over the years sketched a life style on the canvas of my heart; a heart that suppressed emotions that was considered to make a man weak. The same heart that now pumps the blood of a warrior is only focused on love and care.

As I began to evolve as my role as a father I could feel the layers of misguided emotions peel away, and I would get surges of energy and motivation. I could feel the transformation as the layers would peel off. My spirit began to feel a little lighter. Sometimes it's hard to explain that particular feeling to those that never experienced it before. I was still a strong man, but now I accepted the fact that I had to face that, those emotions are necessary for complete proper growth and development. I realized that it didn't compromise my manhood by having those feelings, and that I didn't have to be hard all of the time. I was in the house with my children all day every day; I had to tap into that side of myself.

In the beginning stages of when I first became a father it was very painful and uncomfortable and trust me when I say…I didn't enjoy it! I guess because it went counter clockwise to my makeup. I was 24 years old and immature to a degree; by tapping into that part of my nature, it helped me to develop as a man. I feel as though if I didn't have a daughter at that time, I still would have been stewing in my ignorance and immaturity. My daughter made me revisit the way that I view females; and as a whole my mentality had to change, and she was the catalyst that catapulted me. I want to reveal the pros of fatherhood, of how it makes us more patient, peaceful, and caring. By doing such things it helps us in many ways of our lives.

Patience was one of the first lessons fatherhood made me come to terms with. I had to be more patient because as a first time, full time father I had to get used to the crying and waking up in the middle of the night. In time, I realized that children have a routine, and you just have to learn it and adapt accordingly. Making the mental adjustment of getting used to my daughters' baby do-dooh and the smell that comes along with it was not easy. However, taking the time to clean and wash her up really well so that she wouldn't get any rashes or irritations were things I knew I had to do because I was her provider. I developed a routine for when she cried to try to get her to stop. I would pick her up and walk around with her, which would soothe her, quiet her down, and put her back to sleep. This situation initially aggravated me, but I had to work with her. There was no one to give the baby to so I was trapped, locked down. Time and repetition fostered new habits that taught me patience.

Another characteristic I was not familiar with was being peaceful. Due to my whole make up and exterior being hard, most will never get past my outside layer. I'm not talking about being a super gangster, but the vibe that I give off, a wise person would detect that I am a no nonsense type of guy. That's just who I am without pulling the gangster card. I've learned that's not how you communicate with children. I was with my daughter day in and day out so I was forced to communicate differently; the armor definitely got peeled away. The aggressive tone and language is not utilized because it has become part of the mental shift. Every day I was in that routine creating new habits I gained peace of mind knowing that I was creating a positive environment for my baby girls.

As a parent, it is second nature to become caring. Fatherhood allowed me to have a new found respect for life. I always say a person who doesn't care about their own life is probably not going to care too much about your life either. So, once you give them something to care for it increases the value of life in general to an individual. My daughter gave me a new outlook on life in general. I have a higher regard for human life, which was bred from the relationship I developed with her. Knowing what I know now, most gang members are not men under control no matter what the situation. Why? Because we ride and die off of other people's shit! Shit that ain't even our problems. We must be daddy to our kids, because our children don't give a shit about a big homee or an OG. All they care about is their daddy. There's a lot of shit that I did in the streets that a nigga' deserves what he got, of which I don't regret. There are some things that I did in ignorance; however, as I began to grow as a man I looked at myself in a different light. I see there is no reasoning in ignorance. There are situations that will arise that reasoning can get you out of, but you can't see it because you're an ignorant motherfucker. A person who knows how to reason will take that same situation and work through it and will not have the thoughts of anger or the urge to react in a violent manner. He or she will deal with it by using mind over matter. So, I have learned that instead of attacking and condemning other people I need to work on cleaning up my own shit.

This can be agonizing because I have been banging since I was 11 years old. I have a lot of learned behavior that I have to delete and replace with positive habits that are healthier mentally, and physically. The road to transformation is bumpy with a lot of twists and turns. The thoughts that have been running through my head, I'm talking about the ones that bring agony and pain to my spirit that keep me up at night that want to come out and play. These thoughts have been suppressed by my new mentality, which have been breeding my new actions, and my new habits. Now, that sounds all good, but one day, the gangster thoughts escaped the cell I had them locked away in. I wind up getting with my "homees" and we had a gathering. There were around 50 of us in the apartment. We had guns everwhere shotguns, rifles, Mack 11, and all types of pistols. We were on our gangster shit communicating in our blood slang rowdy as hell and drinking brew. I had a Mossberg in one hand and my daughter in the other, and this was on video. This was on the "Soldiers of Darkness" documentary. Reflecting back on that time when I relapsed I was at the pinnacle of my ignorance. My soul was in agony, and my hands drenched in blood.

When I look back at that night's footage I realized how far I have come. Looking at the raw uncut footage I see myself in the camera saying "Fuck my enemies and K's up," while holding the baby in my arms. As I grow I'm starting to see the results of my changes both mentally and emotionally, which allow me to make better decisions for myself and my family.

I had taken an oath prior to having my daughter to always ride for my "Homees." It was a universal gang oath that I was obligated to, and that's nothing to play around with. Under the oath it's mandatory that you ride for your "Homees" and I was true to the oath. You don't sit around and talk about it "you ride." Now, I have an obligation as a father and family man. At this time my mind and spirit are in conflict, and I'm wrestling between the two. In the world that I grew up in and spent most of my life in I'm supposed to be in the streets tearing up some ass, but that obligation jeopardizes my family and puts them in harm's way. By not going along, it may appear as though I'm not staying true to the code, or true to my homees, but everyone knows the work that I have put in. That was truly a mental hell that I was dealing with, it's rough, painful, and agonizing. Now that I have grown in wisdom, I look back and think about "The Oath" and ask myself, does it mean that I have to ride for a homee's ignorance?

I'm happy I had a girl first. She saved my life! Raising a girl is different than raising a boy. A girl will make you suffer humility, which may not be so much for a boy. A boy will not allow you as much room to tap into certain areas of yourself that you should do compared to a girl. A boy helps you to continue the male masculine gene of being tough, instead of dealing with emotions which leads to having no emotions. One day my daughter was running and she fell. I went to console her, and I remember how I was holding her in my arms and how talking to her made her feel better, and stop crying. If I had a son I probably would have told him to get his ass up. However, with a girl you can't do that, so I learned to become more patient, and nurturing as opposed to being firm and aggressive.

If I would have had a boy first I would have dressed him in all red and I would have taught him the life of a gangster. That would have eventually led to my demise. I am stressing that my daughter taught me a lot, which all came from a sacrifice. I remember reading to my daughter when I didn't want to and how aggravating it was. Now, I am reaping the rewards years later! As I would read to my daughter we connected in many ways and it helped us to bond. We had fun and I read many stories to her that she enjoyed. You can see how her learning at home helped her transition into school. The foundation was set now because we were reading and interacting with her at home. She went into school with a boost of confidence. It was not only beneficial to my daughter but also to me because I was learning at the same time.

I remember a book that was given to me from a loved one on raising girls, and it was talking about flossing, washing their faces and cleaning behind their ears. I was really into this book and I found myself implementing what I learned from the book into my own life. These types of exchanges with my children are developing and helping to cement our bond. To this day my daughter will come into the room and jump into the bed and ask me to read to her even though she is a capable reader. As she progresses in school the words are becoming bigger and more complicated. When I begin reading she listens and reads along picking up on unfamiliar words, and she would take it from there.

As time went on I realized that spending time with my children and watching their shows was having an effect on me. I found myself singing the song it's like I heard it so much that the melody was sketched in my head. I knew something was going on when I was humming the melody when my daughter was not around and the show wasn't on. Change is good! An example of what it would be like if I had a son first, I would have been dressing him in red every day, and I would have been really hard on him, really gangster on his little ass. That's how I would have bred him without any question, and that would have been a disaster because the first couple of years of a child's life are the most influential.

It always starts with people, places, and things. I notice now that when I was younger the environment that I lived in definitely had an effect on me. It helps to shape and mold the individual directly or indirectly, positively or negatively. As I analyzed the people that I was around I noticed that most never went outside of their neighborhoods or their cities. I noticed that in Phoenix and also in New Jersey most "Kats" are trapped in a box and that's all that they know; because that's all that they see due to a lack of exposure. Homees in the hood don't take trips or go on vacation. It always starts with people, places, and things.

Therefore, I have rededicated my life to my family and I am changing to break that generational curse. I have learned that vacations are healthy for my family and I. The more I expose my family to a better way of life the more they can expand and think outside of the box with no limitations. I remember when I took my family to Myrtle Beach, S. C. they loved it so much, and they had lots of fun in the water. We had the inner tubes that we put the children in and guided them around the waterfalls they loved it! The more I do the more I learn, the more they smile and it's the smiles and the hugs that help me get through the hard times and challenges. It also brings about a feeling of accomplishment when I go to my children's school for a daddy and daughter's breakfast or dinner and all of the different activities that come up throughout the year.

Being in that environment and participating in different events are rewarding and therapeutic to me. It also gives my daughters that extra boost and motivation. As I look back and see how unwilling I was to be with my children at the beginning stages of parenthood, and now, I see that my investment of time into my daughters has paid off. I have placed a seed that is growing and taking on a life of its own. I love to see that my children love to learn. My daughter knows over 100 words in sign language that are in the American Sign Language System (A.S.L.). She knows some Swahili and also speaks Pig Latin.

My daughter learns quickly and is very perceptive. She aces all of her spelling tests, and if she hears something one time she picks up on it. She spells and reads fluently, and all of her teachers acknowledge the fact that she is extremely gifted. She loves to learn and at this stage in her life she is anchored in academics, and is excelling in the fundamentals. Therefore, it's a plus that she has athletic ability that is higher than the average.

Being a daddy has its rewards, conversely it has its hardships too. Sometimes I say to myself, I don't want this responsibility, and I don't want people counting on me. Why? Because ultimately I don't want to let anyone down, it pains me because I think I will be taken away. Therefore, I start the process over again in my head, and I know that this is the same force I must fight because I don't want to leave them again. They are precious, innocent, and they need me.

Fatherhood and marriage do not always coincide with the lifestyle of a high profiled gang member. Jiwe was ripping and running in the streets in order to chase fame, and money, but I thought I was doing all of this to provide a better foundation for my family. I was trying to hide away my family in the safety of the Georgia suburbs, while I traveled so I could continue capitalizing on the public figure I had become. However, these two worlds couldn't coincide because at some point, the lifestyle of the streets pulls you back into its trap and can cause you to lose those who mean the most to you. In my world, I later learned that there was nothing more important to me than Neina and my four children. At some point, I would have to choose one over the other.

# CHAPTER 3

Relocating my family to Atlanta was a dream come true. It signified a new beginning and a fresh start. In Atlanta, I was able to be a good father, and a supportive husband. I was a well-rounded family man. However, in order to maintain this new lifestyle, I had to fly back to Newark on several occasions to participate in speaking events. During one particular week, I flew back for a week's worth of events at the Borgata in Atlantic City, University of Pennsylvania and Delaney Hall. It was supposed to be a week to fulfill my professional responsibilities so that I could provide for the life I had built in Georgia.

I was riding in car with two buddies. We just came from the studio and I decided to get some Chinese food from a nearby restaurant. I get out and as I'm walking up to the door two males were walking towards me. At this point my antennas went up because it was somewhere around 10 p.m. at night on Bloomfield Avenue and I see these two males approaching me. As I get ready to make my entrance into the Chinese store, I hear, "hey you know what time it is?" At this point I try to make eye contact with the two individuals but they are extremely close to me so I couldn't really make out their faces. One had a hoodie on so it made it especially difficult to identify his face. I pulled back for a second and he repeats the statement again. "You know what time it is, give it up." Immediately my instincts kicked in and I lunged at the shorter male of the two and we began wrestling. I'm thankful that his comrade was a sucker because he was really just being a spectator and watching and hoping that his friend would get some separation between the two of us. In the mist of the tussle, I was able to get my hands around a pistol and in the in the midst of the chaos, the gun went off shooting the guy who tried to rob me. It went off twice at that point. I just watched him fall. I made eye contact with his friend, but he took off running up the street so I did the same thing and I ran across the street to get away from the situation. From there I was arrested and charged with attempted murder. I was locked and transported to Essex County Correctional Facility.

The entire time this was happening, I could not believe I was in this situation and part of me was going in slow motion. All I wanted to say to the two men was do you know how I am? Like why you trying to rob me? However, everything occurred so fast and instantaneously and just like that everything had changed. I had come to Newark on business and had come back to continue the work that I have been doing for years which was to inspire, motivate and encourage people and here I was being arrested for an attempted murder charge. This incident was an example of how my old life would come to haunt me even when I was trying to engage in positive endeavors.

My family had only moved to Atlanta for two months and all of a sudden our world came crashing down. I was locked up in Essex County Jail for several months trying to figure out how I would be bailed out and prove my innocence. In the meantime, my wife was struggling and trying to figure out what to do financially. The bills were mounting, lawyers had to get paid and bail money had to be gathered. Eventually, I was able to be bailed out and learned that my family had lost the house, the car, the brand new furniture and everything else I worked so hard for.

My dream home in Atlanta was gone and all of our money continued to pay for lawyer's fees and fighting a very draining court case. We had to move to Pennsylvania with Neina's family so that I could stay close to Newark for court dates, but be far enough away so I would not be caught up in any other trouble. I fought my case from the streets. It took a whole year before this case went to trial. The trial experience was extremely draining and stressful. Most of the year was spent in turmoil trying to determine if I would be spending the rest of my life in prison. When I looked over in the court audience, I saw a man that I had met 10 years earlier. I was standing there facing 81 years and shocked to see another old face like mine, but he never looked up at me. The moment was uncanny. I never felt a still moment like this and couldn't fix my lips to speak, but it jerked plenty emotions from everything inside of me. The trial lasted for four days and the victim that took the stand said he did not recognize me and I was found not guilty on all seven counts. I could have went to prison for 81 years, but I was relieved to learn that I was a free man.

Once the trial was over, I was left to pick up the pieces and figure out ways to provide for my family. I worked extremely hard and tried to book several speaking engagements, rebuild my name and network so that I could regain financial stability. Things did not change overnight. Eventually, I was able to move my family back to Atlanta. We took small steps and rented in the beginning. All of this was a huge blow to my ego and I felt extremely embarrassed. Here I was, a man who came from nothing, was given everything and in an instant lost it all. However, I did not let the disappointment overpower my drive to rebuild what we lost. My main concern was to provide my children, wife and mother with all of the amenities they had before. I refused to be a failure.

This situation made me realize some important aspects of my life. For years I appreciated the gangster lifestyle and lived for the adrenaline pumping through my veins twenty-four hours a day, seven days a week and for weeks on end. The pounding in my ears, and my heart racing about a hundred miles an hour, the whole nine was what my life was engulfed in. Teamwork for me was five homees robbing an L-

Q. When I was in the streets, I was in heavy. However, I am now a changed man, but the streets are in my blood. If it was not for my family, some get back, pay back and murder would definitely be on my mind especially in a situation where two men tried to victimize me and ended up turning my world upside down. This transformation from handling things in the street to trying to lead a conventional life can get lonely because I do not feel that anyone can understand the struggles I undergo inside my head.

Today, I am strong and much more confident in my decision making, however, at times I fear myself because of the violence that I am capable of. I do not want to hurt anyone, but there is still anger and revenge in my heart. Each day is a struggle not to lose control and act violently which in reality is second nature to me because of the many years I was surround by it. Despite all of these inner battles, my family and success continues to be my focus as I push forward to rebuild all that has been destroyed by one night.

# CHAPTER 4

"A man cannot serve two masters," this is a quote from the Bible. For years I thought I could. I thought I was different, a child of the streets. I tried to keep my family separate from the gangbanging. I thought I was the exception but that reality came crashing down one afternoon and showed me there are no exceptions, you can't walk with a foot in both worlds and expect them not to destroy one another. I thought I could still hang with people I grew up with, stay out drink with them but a mentor of mine told me that I drank to dumb myself down so that I could step back to that level, which I should have left behind. When he told me this, it made me mad because I wasn't only a product of the streets I had become the streets. This was the one world in which I walked. To suggest that I forget where I came from or who I was, it was not an option. He told me it's not forgetting who you are or where you have come from but moving on to better things for yourself, and some of the people in your life don't want to see that. They want to keep you at the level they are at never changing never evolving. He said that the other world I lived in was the one as a husband, a father, and a man trying to make a difference in the world. Trying to be legit. These two worlds cannot coexist. I always thought that I was different that I could make it happen. It took me years after that conversation before I realized how wrong I had been.

My life has been filled with lessons one of the biggest lessons was forgiveness. As I look back, there was a particular event that showed me that life was more than respecting the code of the streets. That night wasn't any different than any other night, it started off simple enough Neen and I had dinner with the kids. We cleaned up afterwards and started getting the kids ready for bed. While Neen took care of the girls' baths, I popped a cold beer, sat down at the computer and logged into my email. The first four or five messages were all spam, I deleted those and then froze. A name on the next message I saw was a name that had haunted me for the past six years. Why would the man I had blamed for a long time for ruining my life be contacting me? At first I was hesitant to open the email, not sure if I should delete it unread or not but a part of me was curious, the last time I had any contact with this person I was standing on top of him watching my little home boy shoot him nine times. Granted I did not know it was him at the time but that incident cost me six months of my life, six months I could never get back. Missing moments in life that every father, every husband should be there for. When I was locked away I blamed a lot of people for my situation but I knew no matter how much I wanted to lay the blame on someone else, in the end I was the one responsible for my predicament. I had tried to walk in two different worlds, one as a Blood gang member and the other as a college receiver for Delaware State University. My junior year was the epitome of a disaster in the making. I was an All American kick returner with NFL scouts showing up just to watch me practice. Me a street kid from Newark could smell the turf of the big stage of playing on Sundays, every kid's dream was about to come true for me except that wasn't the case. My other life wouldn't allow it.

One night things went wrong, so very wrong! Members of my gang had an altercation with some of my teammates; it all came to a head one night. During that confrontation my teammate Will was shot, it was dark that night I had no idea this night would result in him being the one laid out on a hospital gurney with nine bullets in him, hell I didn't even know he was there. He and I never had any issues. He was a defensive back from Florida, we went against each other every day in practice. The next day when I heard it was him who had been shot I just sat there in shock and said to myself "not Will!" Those bullets had been meant for someone else, someone who had been involved in the friction from the very beginning. I plead out to a lesser charge, Will never showed up to testify against me which I'm sure left the prosecution with little choice but to offer a deal. Those six months changed my life. When you are locked up twenty three hours a day with nothing but your thoughts your life has to change. Some people become bitter and blame the world for their choices, others find religion, whereas some just take a good long look at their life, you might say I did a little of them all.

During my incarceration I began writing as a way to cope with the reality of my situation, just thoughts, parts of my life from when I first joined the bloods as a kid to where it had all led me. At times when I would re-read what I had wrote I realized that it had not been a pretty life at times but it was mine and the choices I had made on my journey had lead me to this little six by nine cell. On my release from the Delaware correction facility the journal I wrote became published under the title "War of the Bloods in my Veins". The next thing I know, I'm in demand. Suddenly, I had people wanting me to make speeches about my life, to talk to young kids. I had found a new calling where I could use my life on the streets to influence people in a positive way. Things were going good. Out of nowhere, I see an email from Will. Memories flooded back from that night in Delaware. It was a terrible situation. Issues we had were with James Edmonds, also known on campus as Game. He was the provoker of the events that night with some of my homees. Game had been provoking me quite a bit days leading up to this events that when I pulled up and realized my fellas had pulled out a pistol on him I was all in. He escaped the house he was hiding in and took off running. Will was with him. We were able to chase them down and unfortunately Will got clipped from one of my guys while Game continued to run into the woods. While Will was down on the ground getting stomped and hit with objects he was then shot 9 times. While he was getting handled, Game was hiding in the woods. It really tripped me out in the aftermath because this was a situation I always hated to see in the streets. Here you have Game calling for reinforcement and Will not even being involved with this issue between Game and I comes to aid him that night but is left for dead.

Days later the paper is released and Game is telling everything, I mean the entire situation from start to finish. I couldn't believe what I was seeing. This guy talked so much garbage about how he from Philly how hard he was and provoked this issue but went straight to police when the hammers got to thumping. Will almost lost his life that night coming to help Game out and this is how it played out. I also thought about how bad I felt because prior to this Will and I were close. Never no beef we practiced hard against each other. While he was down getting stomped I never knew it was him.

"Hey Neen, come here, check this out."

"What up?" she asked as she leaned over me.

"Not sure, trying to decide if I should open it or just delete it."

"Just delete it, you know you can't have any

contact with him, the court ordered that."

Neen was right, but for so long I wanted to reach out to Will, let him know my side of the events that occurred that night, but the state made it quite clear that doing so would get me violated and have me sent back to prison. As much as I wanted to have my say in the matter, there was no way I was going back to jail over it.

"Yo Neen the court said I couldn't contact him but this is him contacting me, don't see how I could get in any trouble for reading it" before she could respond I opened the email.

> *I was sitting here thinking of the best way to write you and I just decided to write directly to you. I have no animosity towards you or any beef and I want you to know I forgive you. I had to forgive in order for me to heal. I am contacting you for closure to the situation for us both and also to say congrats on everything you are doing. I heard you had a book*

*out but I didn't pursue to check until a friend of mine purchased it in a Barnes n noble bookstore. I hope and pray you will respond and again I forgive you and congrats on everything.*

*Sincerely Will*

For too many years I blamed Will for my situation but I knew that wasn't right. Although the bullets weren't meant for him, they were meant for someone else, if they had hit their intended target my situation would not have been any better, what I had never given a second thought to was how that night had affected Will's life and the final line of the email "I forgive you" stunned me. This man felt the spirit driving him to contact me so that we could both move forward and he wanted to talk.

"Could be a trap" that's my Neen always watching out for me.

"Yeah could be but I don't think it is, I think he really reaching out trying to make peace with it all, I think he and I both need that, think it could be a good thing"

"Just be sure to check with your lawyer before you make any contact with him. I ain't saying he ain't on the up an up but no reason to take any chances that we don't need to take."

"And if everything is on the level?"

"Then you got to do what you got to do, you know I got your back," she gave me a kiss and went off to finish the dinner dishes I leaned back and read the email over again, my thoughts roaming as the words sank in.

The next morning I checked with my lawyer Joe Hurley, I got the ok. So I immediately shot back a short response telling him I would like to set up a phone conversation as there were things I wanted him to know not only about that night but how it had affected my life, both negatively and positively. For a few days we exchanged emails and then set up a call, it was one of the hardest calls I've had to make. Although the emails were all very positive, I knew in the back of my mind that the phone conversation could turn at any moment but I also knew that in my heart that I had to talk with him to be able to move on, this chapter of my life had to be put behind me and there was only one way to do that.

"Can I speak to Will"

"This is him"

"Yo bro it's Jiwe"

Will and I talked for a while. We discussed what happened that night and how it had changed both of our lives. I knew the effect it had on my life, but I have to admit I never gave much thought to how that night might have affected him. He had gone through about 6 months of rehab to get back to normal, several surgeries and nightmares, not being able to sleep. He said he would relive the night he got shot in his dreams, waking up in a cold sweat. Crazy to say, him in a hospital bed six months while I'm in a prison bed, and we both waking from our sleep in cold sweats. He said one day when he woke he realized that he had to forgive me for my part in that night in order for him to be able to make peace with it and move on with his own life. Like Will, I had relived that night many times while I was locked up, I was angry that I was behind bars missing my life, I was angry with a lot of people but most of all at myself for putting myself in that position.

Will said a friend had told him about my book War of the Bloods and he had picked up a copy and that is why he decided to contact me. We talked about the things I was doing in the hood, working with kids trying to get them to find a better way, a less violent way. He told me that he was working on a book of his own as he had been talking to church groups and kids giving testimonies about his life and that night and asked me if I'd be willing to write the foreword to it, which I agreed to do.

It was during this conversation that I realized the opportunity that Will and I had to not only change a vicious cycle of black on black violence and retaliation but to show others that we all have a choice, that we could be a part of the power of forgiveness. Too many times in my life I have seen the circle of violence continue to turn because people were not big enough to put the past behind them. Gangs fighting over beef that started before most of the members were even born. Will and I had the opportunity to change that, we had a chance to tell a story, one that needed to be told with a much different outcome. We had the opportunity for a peaceful ending. As we hung up the phone I knew that a friendship I thought was dead had a chance to be reborn.

Over the next few months Will and I would talk on a regular basis, we both planned to get together, I told him I would fly him to New Jersey but he said his family wasn't too comfortable with that, although I didn't like that response I understood it, he had friends and family that didn't trust me because of that night. If the meeting was to take place then it would have to be on mutual ground, amazing that even as we both tried to find peace many of the people around us told us it wasn't possible but I knew that we had to prove them wrong. It was the only way to show the world that we could change it, one person righting one wrong at a time.

After several attempts to get together that fell through for one reason or another, a situation presented itself that was perfect. Orlando, Florida, home to the junior Olympics in which my daughter would be running in, just a few hours from Will. I told him the dates I would be down and we decided that we would get together. We had done as much talking on the phone and internet as we could but we both knew the face to face had to happen before moving on could. Words can be twisted online or over the phone, but when you look a man in the eyes and talk from the heart that is when the truth is laid out for all to see.

After Dashana's run in the junior Olympics, I headed over to the restaurant that Will and I had agreed to meet at. I walked in and he was standing there with his friend Bob, a writer who was working with him on his book which was to be called A Tough Call, I knew Bob through a few emails and phone conversations as he had made contact with me checking different aspects of the book that dealt with me in order to make sure he was portraying me accurately. We all exchanged greetings and then sat down. Will had brought his two young daughters to the meeting as well, which was added confirmation that he was sincere. We talked for about an hour, topics were covered from that night to how Dashana had done on the track. At the end of it I invited them all back to our hotel for a cookout.

As the steaks cooked on the grill I watched as our children played together a sight I never thought I'd see, it just reinforced the belief that if him and I could put our past behind us and build a friendship, so much positive could come from what we had been through. We both had put ourselves into that situation that night and were both to blame for certain aspects of it, but seeing our children playing together, very unaware of what their fathers had gone through made me very glad I had answered Wills email, I was first hand witnessing the circle of hate being broken.

After Will left I found myself going back over

the different events that had brought us both to this moment in our life. I couldn't believe after all that had happened to him he had mustered up the will to forgive me. That day alone changed my outlook on getting over being violated because this man was able to forgive me after almost losing his biggest possession on earth, that being his life.

**Neina's Story**

The first time I saw him he had my full attention. I was never the type of girl to approach a guy so I would have never said a word. So many things were against my rules when it came to him. I told myself when I went to school, no athletes, no super popular guys, matter of fact no real relationships just focus and graduate. Then my frat brother had a Mike Tyson fight night and all those rules went out the window. He sat in a chair away from everyone just observing. There was so much going on but I kept getting distracted by him, the only one not doing anything. I offered him a drink, asked him if he was ok, little did I know I met the man that would father all my children and be my husband. He was a man of little words which kept me interested.

We finally spoke the next day through my line sister Nicole, and found out even though we were opposite in personality we had so much in common. Things I told him about my childhood he would have never thought. The biggest thing was we had the same goals in life. We both wanted children, family etc. It was crazy. Honestly the first night we kicked it we have been together every night since. We were like best friends immediately.

As time went on I learned Dashaun had many different layers to him. I learned how to handle each one. I think this is what captured his heart, is my patience learning how to handle him. He is so rough and tough on the outside, but so fragile and almost innocent on the inside.
This is what I fell in love with. I always saw this great man inside of him. He was sweet and innocent to a certain extent. The exterior the other people saw was a result of all of his hurt and pain. His temper is what caught him the charges he has. His rage is very difficult to know how to handle.

So four years later and now I am Lady Jiwe. Crazy but I hated that name because I hated Jiwe. I love Dashaun, Machete stole my heart, but I hated Jiwe. Crazy isn't it? Well let me tell you why. Jiwe is the complete opposite of both Machete and Dashaun. He is a cheater, a liar, arrogant and selfish person. We all know the saying "You couldn't walk a mile in my shoes". This saying is true without any exaggeration what so ever. It wasn't easy. You have to deal with a man that has power, sexy as hell, a public figure that people think have all this money, and an all-around fun person. He has always had female friends a lot of them. So that was another thing to get used to.

When you have someone in the spot light women want them more. It's like a challenge to them. I was so naïve. I was the type of woman that if you had a girl I didn't want anything to do with you. I naturally thought all other women were the same. Being Lady Jiwe takes patience, trust, and persistence. I am going to elaborate on all three. Patience plays a big part. You have to have patience to deal with feeling like you come second to the streets, fans, social media, homies, etc. There were a lot of times he was away more than home. Then when home so exhausted still didn't see him. That's one thing about him when he is dedicated to something he goes hard and gives his all. So you have to have patience dealing with someone like him. The mood swings, the depression, the rage, the public eye, the pressure. It's a lot. I had to keep him up on his medication for the anxiety and depression. His rage is nothing like I have ever seen before. That's what all the fans never get to see, when he crashes, what I'm left putting back together. You can't be demanding because you have to remember how demanding the public is of him and this is what can potentially make y'all rich one day. Just hang in there is what you have to tell yourself. When you see women flirting with your man on social media publicly and you know they know about you, you have to be the bigger person and not respond to the ignorance. It's hard, but remember this is chess and not checkers. It's funny, I don't even like chess but I mastered it in this area of my life.

Trust……… a small word that holds a lot

of weight in any relationship. Once it's gone it's so hard to get back and once you get it back you can lose it so quickly. One thing I admired about Dashaun is be careful what you asked because he was a very honest person and would tell you the truth. Jiwe stole that person from me. Trust was a thing I fought day in and day out to have with my marriage. I wanted my perfect family that we talked about for hours on the phone. I would ignore those gut feelings, females smiling in your face trying to get to know you, not cause they want to befriend you but to see what it is about you that got him. Trust me I saw straight through a majority of these females talking about sis and queen. I would play the role and play dumb but I was always on point. I have yet to be wrong. So trust is huge. Trust that you have enough fight to hold on to the end. And trust that you will not let these bimbo bitches win. That will get you through.

Finally, persistence. If you want something bad enough you will fight and never stop. Trust me the fame, the women, I knew it would get old after a while. I was persistent to have my family. I was persistent to have that man I saw and held in my arms so many nights as he cried. Persistence to help develop this awesome man. Persistence to stand by him no matter what legal situation, what infidelities and outside pregnancies, what looked like no bouncing back, persistence to do whatever needed to be done to fulfill our dream. You never give up on someone or something that you want. The man I have today is the Dashaun I fell in love with thirteen years ago. I knew he would come out one day; he just had to fight his demons. It takes a village to raise a child and a strong woman to develop a man out of a lost boy.

The event that could have taken him away from me and our unborn child for years, I remember the night like it was yesterday. That night changed our lives forever. We fought through it, it showed him how I really had his back and I was in his corner. The thing that messed with him is the man that got hurt he was cool with. He had no problems with him at all. They played football together they were cool. I remember during the case Dashaun wanted to reach out to Will just to let him know he would never cause any harm to him intentionally. It bothered him a lot. He just wanted to let him know that. A lot of times it's his anger and rage that gets him into situations. Once everything calms down, Dashaun is a very rational person. He kept talking about just trying to let him know there was no bad blood. Of course I had to talk him out of doing this, it could have actually made his case worse and we didn't know how Will's family was going to react at that time.

Years go by, Dashaun's book comes out which talks about the incident, and we are carrying on with our lives. Then about a year or so after his book comes out Dashaun tells me he spoke to Will. Of course I am like Will who? He quickly reminds me and my mouth was just open I was shocked, how did y'all get in contact what did y'all say come on give me all the details. He tells me about their conversation. As I am sitting there watching him I see a smile on his face as if he was relieved. I know that was eating at him all these years that Will thought Dashaun would want to hurt him. I know it felt good for him to be able to give his side of the story. I know that meant a lot. Regardless of the picture people tried to paint of Dashaun, he is a really big hearted loving person. He cares how people view him, he really doesn't like to be looked at as a monster.

So they spoke. It allowed Dae to get some relief and I was happy with that. I figured that would be it, maybe follow each other on social media. Then he comes and tells me he going to meet Will in person. His safety is always my first priority, and I didn't like the idea at all!!!!! All kinds of thoughts went through my head. What if they try and set him up. What if they want pay back? I really didn't want him to go at all. I wanted to go but I knew that was out of the question.

The meeting with Will made me especially

nervous cause Jiwe was going to him. It wasn't like they were meeting on neutral grounds. To be honest, I wasn't really thinking Will would do anything, but I know his boys were not feeling it and he has no control over what they do. Not everyone was on the same level that Jiwe and Will were on. All these things are running through my head as Jiwe walked out the door but I don't want to say anything, this is a pure moment that should not be ruined. But I had my concerns. He had been wanting to close this chapter of guilt in his life and I didn't want to steal that from him. I have a habit of being a worry wart and that causes problems with us sometimes. But then again when you have lived the life that we have it comes with the territory. Of course I see him off with a kiss. I love you, and Morris family. It kills me every time he is out working towards his passion which is saving our young men, trying to make a change, and making a name for himself. I picture that being the last time I see him. It's bitter sweet. I know he is serving a good purpose and his heart is in the right place, but niggas not bout nothing and ain't never gonna' be shit want to take that from people. I saw it. So many of his homies were like this but he just didn't want to hear it and unfortunately a lot of them proved me right.

I get text of his every move. A rule we have is to always know whereabouts and who's with you. At all times no matter how far apart we may be I know where and who he with. He texted me he was there. Let me know it was him and the man he wrote his book with named Bob. So I reply just make sure you stay in touch. He does, which eases my mind. He keeps assuring me everything's cool and that they just really talking and getting everything understood. I could imagine the feeling for Dashaun. He was probably so relieved to get his point across. He calls when they done to let me know everything went well and the next time we go to Orlando for track they want the families to meet.

A year later we had a track meet to go to in

Orlando for our oldest daughter Dashana. Dashaun has kept in touch with Will so of course it's only right that the families meet. It sounds all good but I had so many feelings about it. It was great that they were able to patch things up and move forward. Women are completely different, we hold grudges, we protect our families, and it's hard for us to forgive once you violate our loved ones, especially our husbands. To be honest I didn't want to meet Will's family, particularly his wife Trina. I didn't want to feel like I was meeting someone that hated my husband and felt like we owed them something. I wasn't beat for the ass kissing. I remember asking Dashaun over and over, you sure they good to come you sure, do you trust this? I remember having my guard up like if I see any type of attitude from her I'm pulling back. See one of the things with me is anyone I meet through my husband I am open and try my best to develop some sort of relationship with them. If he is introducing them to me that means they are important to him and he loves them. He is very selective who he allows me to meet and who he knows. So I meet his wife Trina, I am very good at picking up vibes, of course I got the feeling she was only doing it to make Will happy, but she was pleasant. They brought all the children and we all went swimming. We made small talk nothing too deep, but I could tell we were different people than what she had in mind. I liked them, I thought they were nice people. After looking back on it, I really think Dashaun and Will could start a serious movement. I feel they could travel this country and tell their story. It's been three years and we still keep in touch to this day. It really is a powerful movement and a story to be told. It really is. I admire Dashaun for always going above the rest, always trying to do what no one else has done. He really is a great guy. He has demons he fights daily but he is really a great guy.

■■■■■■■■■■■■■■■■■■■■■■■■■■■■■■■■■■■■■■■■■■■■■■■

# CHAPTER 5

Death and destruction were something that I had become accustomed to. However, this new life afforded me opportunities that many people from where I come from will never experience. My trip to Africa was the highlight of my career. Africa was just the beginning for me. I have a generation of youth that looks up to me. I do not want to be another statistic or a what could or should have been story.

Since my first book, I learned that America has a fascination with the gangster and criminal lifestyle. This infatuation has opened several doors for me and allowed me to embark on life changing experiences. One such encounter was to meet a kindred spirit that grew up in similar violence a world away. I met Ishmael Beah through a documentary on the Sundance channel I was featured in called "Brick City". Ishmael was a child soldier in Sierra Leone and spent his youth surrounded by violence and destruction. He was trained to fight with rebels and was rescued by UNICEF in his teens. As soon as we met, we understood each other. Although we were from different continents, we were the same age and as children, we were forced into a life of chaos due to the dangerous world around us. I invited Ishmael to the streets of Newark where I spent much of my youth. He learned about the American gang life through my eyes. Speaking about our experiences made me understand that both of us were child soldiers that survived the war of the streets we grew up in. We both held a great burden on our shoulders because we were both regarded as leaders of our community and our fame provided us a platform to be the representative voice for those who share our traumatic experiences.

Ishmael invited me to stay with him in Africa. I took the 16 hour trip and finally made it to the motherland. Things got tense immediately as soon as I exited the plane. People were very aggressive towards me in trying to help with my bags, asking if I needed transportation and providing anything they could to make some money. It was overwhelming to say the least. In fact, one man was talking to me, trying to get me to pay for some assistance with bags, I agreed. I paid him some American money and that was a big mistake, three other men all closed in on him demanding the money. I thought to myself, damn not here even ten minutes and it's going down. My stay in Africa was humbling. I wanted to live life as they did. I observed them fetch water, fish in the Atlantic and used my time there to just take in their culture. It's something that I've understood even as a little black boy that we should all take at least one trip to Africa, and here I was, finally making the voyage.

Ishmael had the most luxurious home compared to everyone else in his village. He provided for a large family that included extended family. He was like a hero to his people and with good cause. Although he was successful in the United States, he made sure that he gave back to his homeland. Things that seem commonplace in America such as running water and electricity are luxuries in the part of the world Ishmael comes from. He provided his village with power and electricity. They revered him and looked to him for leadership. Similar to what I was to my people. We gave our people hope. The idea that dreams can come true. It was amazing to watch great grandmothers working side by side with their great great grandchildren fetching water, cleaning chicken and doing laundry. I mean the whole village got their days started faithfully early in the morning. Everybody was working hard for what was to come to them during the day. It made me see how ruined we are in America. We train our kids just to send them away for college so that they then can build a new family. I do not like this idea. I loved the idea of how there were a few hundred people and 5 generations of family in one village. Although they had very little, their life was radiant. Their respect for their elders was what surprised me the most because elders were treated like royalty. Here in America, people look down on old people. We in the states feel like the elderly are washed up with little to no use, whereas here in Africa the elders were the most respected. They had story time where the elders would sit around a fire and tell stories to the great grands and they would soak up all the wisdom.

What I was not ready for was how Africa really impacted children. I mean there were so many amputees everywhere. Many of them were victims of the civil war with lost limbs to prove it. But they just lived their lives as if it never happened. The children played in filthy muddy water with pigs and feces. Half of them didn't even wear shoes and some were naked for the day. Sometimes, watching their quality of life brought tears to my eyes. Everywhere I went the people latched on to me as if I was some big celebrity. I could see in their eyes that many of them stopped dreaming. Defeat was written all over them. They were literally like the walking dead and this ripped me apart. I wanted to do so much for them. Yes poverty is real in Newark and the states but nothing compared to what I was witnessing here in Sierra Leone. Watching the kids play in mud really made me see how spoiled our children here in America are. They complain about everything whereas these kids made the best of the little they had. There were no demands from kids to have the latest Nikes or a certain brand of clothes so that they would fit it, for them it was about getting that next meal.

Too many times I have witnessed first-hand what the love of money can do and the evil that comes with it. People die in Newark trying to take what others have. Here, this is not a problem because everyone has the same thing, which is nothing. It really hit home with the idea that I had always known that I was blessed but taken so much for granted. This trip made me realize that family is the most important thing. I know very few people that could live in the conditions that I was witnessing and be content or happy, but I witnessed people doing just that. Their life was a daily struggle for survival for the bare basics. People were not beefing over the imaginary boundary lines of two feuding hoods instead they were fighting to protect themselves in an all-out war. Neither situation is one that any rational person would choose to be in and both offered too much opportunity for death to knock on your door at any given moment and take the most precious thing you have in this world that being your life.

Staying with Ishmael helped me realize how men from our background can never truly be healed from the devastation of our past. We both spend a lot of time being aware of our surroundings and watching our back. Trust is not easy for either one of us. Before he went to bed, I could hear him checking if all doors and windows were locked. Similar to me, I knew he had trouble sleeping because I could hear his footsteps in the middle of the night. Before we would enter his estate, he would circle the perimeter of his home to make sure there were no trespassers or tails. Although he never explained his paranoia, I understood him because I live my life the same way. Growing up and seeing the things we did has had a lasting impression on both of our minds. Our story brought us together, but our history helped us to create a silent bond of understanding.

I did feel envious of Ishmael even though I admired him as well. Like me, he was a leader for his people. They respected him because he survived the war and when we would walk through his village, you could tell people were extremely proud of him. Although we were around some dangerous people, I even saw 12 year olds with AR 15's, I never felt as if they were envious of him or wanted to hurt him in any way. We both shared this responsibility and obligation to take care of our people because we had been given opportunities that others will never gain access too. Even though I took care of my people and tried my best to appease everyone around me, I did not feel the same love reciprocated towards me that I felt Ishmael received from his people. Watching Ishmael made me realize you did not have to buy happiness from your people because if they really love you, they would honor you for yourself. Everyone around Ishmael was supportive.

I longed for that same sense of encouragement and support from my friends. However, I never felt genuine love from my people as I felt here in Ishmael's surroundings. In regards to all those I considered family, I felt obligated to take care of them all because I had been given opportunities they weren't. I could feel the envy from my surroundings on several occasions and instead of distancing myself, I dug deeper into my generosity and took them more places. I bought them more things almost as if I was trying to buy their love. I was always genuine and just couldn't understand why the same sincerity was not reciprocated. I couldn't understand how they could feel a certain way towards me for me working hard and gaining success. I always felt as if I had to give to receive and once I had nothing to give, the love would run out.

The trip to Africa filled a void in my soul and reawakened my spirit. I saw genuine love, happiness and support. These were the feelings I longed for from my environment and looked towards the streets in hopes to receive this type of sincere emotion. Instead, I was met with envy, disappointment and abandonment. My experience in Ishmael's homeland exposed me to what my life was lacking in the gang life that I had valued so highly. I brought back these lessons and knew I needed to fill this void in order for me to be content in my life.

## CHAPTER 6

Public service announcement to the streets!!! I dedicated 22 years of my life to you. You had me by the balls. You controlled my entire life. I played by all of yours rules. I was a straight "A" student in the school of "hard knocks". You pledged many of us to take an oath to play by rules and codes that you constantly changed without notice. I lived my life worshipping your values and principles but realize what you showed me was just fool's gold. Everything you taught me was everything to kill me. I have had so many horrendous nights trying to love you. You have given me nothing but sadness and pain. I watched my first friend die in your playground at 11 years old. You have taken 33 of my friends. Only a few escape your stronghold and the many that still walk with you try to numb their pain as if they are walking zombies. They are out here high off of multiple pills and various drugs just waiting to die. Every time I think of you, you bring tears to my eyes. The lifestyle I lived in your grasp had me in a spell as if I was stuck like a deer in headlights. I felt as if I had no other option and I was trapped without any exits. I seriously hope and pray this new generation leaves the checker board alone and learns to push them chess pieces. Every time I hear the young guys brag about you, promote you, it hurts me to my heart because I know what they cannot see. I am feeling what they will eventually feel...disillusionment.

Thirty-three of my friends have died. I started seeing these deaths as young as eleven years old. These reminders haunted me as I entered the funeral of my friend Dame. Just a few weeks ago, I tried my best to convince Dame to come down to Atlanta with me. He and I had discussed getting out of the streets on several occasions and going to Georgia to start over seemed like the perfect plan. He even agreed to come down, but he wanted to work and save up money before coming down. My heart was heavy with grief knowing that had he just come down, he would still be alive. Seeing Dame's body hit me like a ton of bricks. I thought about our conversations and times that we spent together, which were slowly running through my head as I began to reevaluate my life; and the things that I was going through and doing at that point in my life. His death served as a reality check. Every homee's death sketches a different imprint in my mind and heart and this one had its own unique signature.

Dame's death was particularly heartbreaking because I knew what he stood for. He was the type of man that despite being involved in the streets, he was into empowering the kids that looked up to him. Dame took so much pride in his health and fitness and tried to instill this same type of discipline to those who were willing to listen to his advice. Although I have lost a lot of good friends to violence, I was still shocked to see such positive person lose his life in the streets due to a bullet. It reminded me again of the close grip the streets had on all of us that lived according to its rules. Even those of us who wanted to better the community or inspire the youngsters looking up to us, could at any moment pay the ultimate price of death. We accept the rules, try to abide by them to the best of our ability and some like Dame, try to make some difference in a positive manner even if is not respected by the streets. However, in this lifestyle, there are no real rewards, just a lot of heartache and consequences, court dates and caskets.

As I'm viewing my homee's body, scanning the room and dealing with my personal emotions, a tear falls down the side of my eye. As I am slowly wiping it away the lyrics from Tupac's "Is there a Heaven for a G" starts rolling through my head and out my mouth:

"How many brothers fell victim to the streets R.I.P. young nigga, there's a Heaven for a G. It will be a lie if I told you I never thought of death, my nigga's we the last ones left. Life goes on!" Every time the hook ends it automatically rewinds and plays again. So as I'm walking around paying my condolences, that's the only thing in my mind. I see people looking at me and speaking to me, but I don't hear their words. Everything is in slow motion. This is the soundtrack of my life.

My feelings jumped in and took over me and transformed into anger and rage, and then I'm back to being grateful that I'm alive. As I'm staring at him I'm saying to myself a lot could have been done differently because it didn't have to end this way. I looked at his mother and saw the same sorrow and anger on her face that my other homees' mothers had. I wasn't able to get to her because she was surrounded by a group of people who were helping her get through this tragedy. I said to myself, I'm happy he didn't have any children because I hate looking at the kids during funerals. It becomes too much for the heart to handle. When I was about 22 or 23 years old I went to three of my homees funerals in one week. This is the order for the week: I went to one on Monday, another on Wednesday, and the last on Friday. Going through that experience as a young man changes you. Most funerals that I have attended in order to pay respect to my homees, I am usually able to detect the different emotions in the room. You can see the family that is mourning at the loss of a family member; they are angry but mostly sad at the loss. Then, you have your homees (the bangers) who are mourning out of anger and want some sort of revenge; you can see that they are pissed off and aggravated. You can see the plots and schemes for revenge in the body language. A blood's war cry is very LOUD. Then, you have the people who are just there for whatever reason. While everyone is in the room going through different emotions I'm saying to myself how long am I going to have nightmares about this. How many days is this going to keep me up at night and how many times am I going to wake up out of my sleep?

Dame's funeral made me reflect on my life. For years I appreciated the gangster lifestyle; the adrenaline pumping through my veins twenty four hours a day, seven days a week for weeks on end. The pounding in my ears, and my heart racing about a hundred miles an hour the whole nine, it was what I lived for. In my transformation from the streets I feel lonely in many things that I do. Maybe this is the way it's supposed to be. It's confirmed daily that my lectures are helping younger people and adults. It's amazing that my lifestyle is what Hollywood & America has a fascination with, another lifestyle that was exploited to make billions of dollars. Misinformation fucked a lot of young people up about the game and their approach to it. I tell them all of the time that gangsters are not machines or animals; however, one can act as such. Gangsters are sufferers. They love, feel, hate, run, bleed, and die. Gangsters can also be giving instead of always taking something or someone. If you really think about it, gangsters owe a lot of people. Looking back to my childhood in Phoenix, I was already walking through the valley of the shadow of death; therefore, today each day is a miracle I'm above ground. Each day is a struggle not to lose control and act violently which is all too easy and second nature.

As I look at the so-called gangsters and at the mentality I realized that in order to evolve to the next level I had to trade in a lot of the myths that the gangster lives by or is supposed to live by. I had to clear up the myths that outsiders have about gangsters. Myth #1 gangsters don't cry. Myth #2 gangsters don't take care of their families. Myth #3 gangsters don't read. Those are just a few of the myths that I know are not true at least for myself. All 3 myths about gangsters mentioned above were necessary elements before my transformation into adulthood and becoming a better husband, father and human being. Gangsters can be really hard and real riders but at the end of the day we are still human. It's amazing how nowadays everyone wants to be a gangster; If not they want to be on some gangster shit, and mean mugging, obscene language super hard, super gangster. Nowadays, I'm directing all of my attention to the younger people telling them that it doesn't pay to be a tough guy because it comes with a price. At the end of the day your family will be suffering. Being at a homee's funeral is proof of this.

The dynamics of a homee's funeral is different than a regular person. Besides the flowers, family, and mourning, there is a heavy police presence. You will notice the presence blocks away and the closer you get the more cars and uniforms you will encounter. They are there to prevent any type of revenge that could occur while the homees are in their huddles drinking and politicking about who is responsible, and who should be looking for those responsible. All of these emotions of revenge, sorrow, death, surveillance overwhelm these types of funerals. They serve as a reminder of how life can be over in an instant. This particular day made me realize how I have become more aware of my surroundings and those who are not necessarily in my inner circle, I'm more cautious of people, places, and things. Being around this despair reminds me that I want to live.

Some may question my intent on living and feeling disillusioned by the streets. Well my answer to them is the following, "Ever just look at yo'self in da mirror? Question is are you happy or displeased? When I look in the mirror I'm not happy. I don't wanna' hear all that all you been thru is yo' testimony crap either. I ain't happy with the things I suffered or been through. However, I have started a new chapter a new book with new memories new choices and outlooks that will override my prior life. But if you ain't got 33 dead homees 4 due to suicide, missed 2 of yo' 4 kids births because you in prison, gave yo' mama grey hair from her worrying if you going make it home at night, watched your childhood friends die every week & eventually get accustomed to it, if you ain't ever slept in cemeteries so that you could still prove to your dead homee you was never leaving his side, if you never played Russian roulette four separate times, if you never prayed to God for strength and accuracy to kill your enemies, if you never dumped five pills along with a 5th of whatever light & dark and then went hunting with three of your killers in a stolen whip and the following mornin' can't remember shit from da night before, if you never been slapped by 5 different moms who came to the hood and slapped yo' face because they felt they left their child in your hands and now he dead, or the fact you haven't avenged his death fast enough, if you never had a mother cry in your arms to help get bail lawyer money for her son that's locked for murder, aggravated assault and robberies, if you never been to a funeral to bury a 14 year old homee of yours and got the whole hood looking to you, waiting, itching for the call to move on the hood that's responsible, THEN DON'T TELL ME SHIT! If you never been to prison locked up 23 hours and 40 minutes a day, and have big racist white CO's in Delaware rushing your cell with the goon squad and beat on you because you control the entire prison, if you never laid in a prison medical bed bleeding internally from the pounding the guards gave you and they won't allow you to make a phone call, won't allow you to get a visit or receive or write mail until you heal I DON'T WANT TO HEAR SHIT!"

Being here at another funeral, another life lost, another person who pledged their oath to the streets and the result again is the same…DEATH!

# CHAPTER 7

"Hey Neen I'm going to the car, hurry up I can't be late to Probation."

"Ok boy I'm coming!"

It is a beautiful day as my wife and I get ready to go check in with my Probation Officer in Georgia. It is May 12, 2014, the day after Mother's Day. We have created a new life in a suburban town, miles away from my past. This new life allows me to be a husband and a father to my four children. It is not the life I grew up living, but it is a life that provides me with self-gratification.

Neen is talking to me as she starts the truck. Within my peripheral, I see a car pull up to the driver side rear of the truck and a face emerges covered with a ski mask with a gun pointing directly at us. Hit! Hit! Hit! I'm being moved on. I tap my waist, no gun. Shit! Everything at this point moves in slow motion. I see another car and then a group of black SUV's pulling up. Members of the U.S. Marshals began hopping out with shotguns, vests, and helmets all screaming, "Hands Up!" I look at Neen for answers and she responds with a blank stare. I see the shock in her eyes and we are both dumbfounded and clueless as to what is happening. As I raise my hands, Neen does the same, I'm wondering what the hell is going on. Immediately, my door is swung open and I'm snatched out and thrown to the ground. Shotgun smashed into my temple, damn, he can finish me right here in front of Neina. Finally, one of the law enforcement agents clues me in as to what is happening. "Mr. Morris you are under arrest for three attempted murders in East Orange, New Jersey." I was taken to the Clayton County Jail. Once I get processed and through orientation they assigned me to my cell. I finally get a moment to gather my thoughts. "What the fuck is going on?"

***Journal Entry Date: May 14, 2014 Clayton County Jail***

I did not want to be in this place again. I

walked out of Delaware Correctional Center on October 31, 2005 because of an incident that changed my life forever. Since then, I was given the opportunity to become a published author, a speaker and a well-known public figure. Life had changed drastically and given me a means to provide new opportunities for myself and my family. As I sit in my cell, I realize that I am currently the property of the state of Georgia. As I write these very words, I am waiting to be extradited to the state of New Jersey on aggravated assault charges along with attempted murder charges. I am locked up in Max with nothing but time so I find myself empty and lonely once again around unfamiliar people. I have worked so hard to leave my old life behind and move forward. The worst feeling in the world is to look in the mirror and cry and hurt from the image you see.

Being locked up allows you to see how strong your mind is. You can only sleep so much in a day, work out so much, play chess, cards, or read. You cannot escape the darkness of just allowing your mind to roam and at some point you have to accept the fact that you are powerless and stuck. When I say I was lost in plain sight what I'm saying is I'm a very visible man, my life is on display for the world, but I am totally lost! I embraced people that I met. I lent a helping hand to people who secretly used me. I loved people who took advantage of my influence, power, and resources. I was lost because growing up I was very confused about my identity. So I learned to create the environment I wanted around me. This gave me life, a purpose to have people need me. I felt validated and useful. I had the wrong people in my circle. I've learnt valuable lessons in trusting people. That's why I can count on one hand how many people I can fully trust. Never again will I open myself up to be taken advantage of. I lost many of whom I consider close friends. I feel my life is being used to go through these hardships to have the stories to tell. I've chosen to be brutally honest about my fears and feelings. It may not lend me any new friends but then again I'm not looking. The fame accumulated never set well with me. When you live a life of a banger, the last thing you want is to have an easily identified face from strangers. This always made me highly uncomfortable and on edge in public. People would approach me from everywhere, driving by in cars. This is the main reason why I always kept a lot of dudes with me. Safety! My anxiety would be off the charts and no one even knew. It definitely takes a certain personality to withstand a certain level of success. I've suffered survivor's guilt and was diagnosed with it in 2007.

People have turned on me, have lied on me and framed me and I still can't understand why all this happened. I'm really hurt and I feel like I'm losing it at the top. I've been there before and I feel like I am really in a demonic war. The devil wants my life. I'm covered in tats to hide the real me. A big part of why I tatted so much because I always felt obligated to represent for the dead. I watched so many years pass by where homees would celebrate our dead homees a strong week tops after that they became a distant memory. I never wanted to forget. I was never comfortable with myself so I became something else or someone. Last night I literally cried myself to sleep. Hands in the air lying on my back, saying, "I surrender. I surrender." I said it so many times I lost count.

During these late nights, I am trying to find peace of mind to replace the heat and misery. I ask God to talk to me every night. Tell me something. I really try to forget the past because the thought of it pierces my insides. It hurts and I ask for forgiveness every day. I wonder when I die, will it matter? I know it will for my family. I thought I moved on from my past, but being here forces you to address your demons and relive memories that you thought you buried away in the furthest part of your soul. Throughout my life, I have been known by various names. The streets knew me as Machete, the public embraced me as Jiwe and I was born with the name Dashaun. However, as I sit in this cell, I am forced to ask myself, who am I today and why did I end up back here.

If I have to answer who I am, I have to revisit all of the events that have made me the man I am today. To start with, let me tell you a tale of a gangbanger that was headed towards hell and destroyed the lives of others on the way. Newark, NJ helped shape the man I am today. I grew up in poverty and was surrounded by an environment occupied by thugs, drugs and crime. I lived in the city that gave birth to the stolen car phenomenon. I lived in a city where the community felt equivalent to quick sand because it was clear that everybody around me was slowly sinking. There are thousands of gang members in Newark, most, if not all neighborhoods are run by gangs. So even if you are not a gang member, but live in a gang related neighborhood, you classified. Not only was this a real problem for the youth in my community, but most of the youth in these poverty-stricken communities lived in single-parent homes. With the lack of a father figure, I clung to the older guys in my community who offered me the male companionship—a father's love—I was missing.

My role models and idols were the most violent guys in the neighborhood. The violence and crime I witnessed hardly affected me or the other kids in the community. In fact, it became the norm and was accepted as a regular part of life. I would drink alcohol daily to ease the pressure, trying to drown out reality. Overtaken by depression, I started having thoughts of taking my own life. There were several nights that were filled with these emotions of hopelessness. Despite the chaos around me and the disarray within me, my life was filled with several divine interventions. I remember on one particular night, I was out looking for a jux so that I could buy some new clothes. I'd damage my inside with my usual killer drink. E&J straight with a shot of gasoline on top. Pop a pill and let my mind go.

I found that I was the only one on the streets. I mean literally every block I turned down, there was no one. It was strange that the streets were empty. It was as if God had intervened on my behalf. As a matter of fact, God has done that on several occasions and being put in this cage again is making me wonder why I was given all of these chances and why was I brought back here.

***Journal Entry Date: May 15, 2014 Clayton County Jail***

A thought that often occurs when I see what stares back at me in my reflection is this body that is all marked up is from the life I've lived. I used to believe my tats were a representation of where I had been and what I've been through which is true but I'm trying to move forward. It disrupts my growth. I have to face my past every day and am always reminded of the pain I've caused and the pain I felt. Every time I look in the mirror my mood is altered by the death in my face. Sometimes I feel that chasing my dreams is the very thing that haunted me. I don't think I was ready nor prepared for it. I enjoyed the power and the influence, but the more I gained, the more I lost. With the exception of my children, wife, and Mama, all others remind me of pain.

I don't know what it's like to be me or be average. From an early age I've been running the show everywhere I have gone. I've never been comfortable in my own skin that stems back to my destructive, unstable, and abusive childhood. In turn, I always found myself reinventing myself because I was always moving to new places and meeting new faces. I really don't have a foundation that belongs to me. The tattoo on my flesh are to cover the pain in me so I guess that confirms the statement hurt people hurt people well I am that person all in one. I have had so many people I have helped in my life and they are the ones that turned on me. I questioned, "how do we abuse the love someone showed us consistently when things get hot?" They crossed me. I think a majority of it is due to jealousy, but what bothers me is I shared all of my success with these guys. I have finally humbled myself to believe all respect ain't worthy. Certain levels I won't go to, but respect can no longer be the pivotal point that determines my actions. This journey to break free of a behavior and lifestyle has been a painful and difficult one. I've been chasing my reputation for far too long trying to maintain what I built up for over 20 years. I realize that was part of my problem. What I had done to build my reputation was never going anywhere. I should have used that time more positively. I should have used that time to focus entirely on who I was presently.

***Journal Entry Date: May 27, 2014 Clayton County Jail***

I spoke to mom and Neen today. Georgia violated me, so I have to go to court for that. Could be 10 days in which I would have time to serve. But the case in Jersey comes first. If I bail out of New Jersey, then I have to sit and wait for

Georgia to come and get me. I just feel like I fear the moments with my thoughts and that's when I'm hurting the most. That's when the tears flow. I'm in a very dark and lonely place and I'm fighting to keep my sanity. I'm really broken in a thousand pieces and what's left I'm trying to repair. Guess I needed this sit down to fully get it.

***Journal Entry Date: May 28, 2014 Clayton County Jail***

Tears came down my face today with mama came to visit. Just couldn't hold them in. I feel lost. She had a lot of positive things to say. I know she loves me and she even feels ministry is in my future. But I don't know if I could teach from the Bible. That would be a challenge. I'm really getting in touch with Dashaun. I still wonder what he's like. Is he tough, funny, sensitive? Neen says that's who she fell in love with. I have to find that guy and get him back. Walking around I feel like a guinea pig in a cage and I'm fighting for freedom.

Time to lock back in. I hate hearing prison cells opening and closing. I feel numb inside. My depression is a place with no cares. I'm like really in a bad mood. I really wanna' go. I'm so close to giving up. I'm so hard! I'm so hard! I have to say to myself. It's so hard to stay positive. I'm tired of the noise. Every sound feels suffocating from the sounds of the cells, the yelling, the keys, the dominos, everything. I just wanna' be home. I'm tired.

Several days later, I wanted to see a doctor because of my mental state. The depression and frustration of being confined were driving me crazy. I needed answers or something to take this pain away. The isolation of prison can become overwhelming and disheartening. Despite looking for help and hope, the darkness and hopelessness began to overtake my spirit. A few weeks prior I was living my dream. I was an official film maker. My movie Deathcoast Str8 Outta Newark just premiered at the AMC theater at NJ garden mall. There was NO questioning my place in the world because I was on top of it (think Leonardo DiCaprio with arms outstretched in Titanic). But on this day though, I was empty. I was questioning my place in the world. I was questioning my place as a father. I was questioning my place in life. I was all alone and I felt it. So, not knowing what to do, I tried to pray. Up to this point in my life, I didn't pray at all. Even though I grew up going to church because when I was younger mama made us, I didn't know much about God and I certainly didn't know how to pray. So, I said, "God, if you're real, I need you to show up. Show me that you give a rip about me and what's going on in my life." The main minister guy on my unit called me asking if I'd be willing to talk about God. Huh? Me?

This man shared that God loved me but that sin separated me from God. He asked me how I was going to overcome this and waited an awkwardly long time for me to answer. I didn't know. Finally, he said that Jesus put himself in my place on the cross so that I could have a relationship with God. He told me I could enter into this new life through faith and get it started with another prayer. I didn't feel comfortable praying with him there. So, I said thanks and he prepared to leave. That's not the moment when my life changed forever. My life changed forever when the man who had brought God into my cell left…but God stayed. From that time, life has never been the same.

Then on one particular day, I heard an announcement over the loud speaker broadcasting a Bible study meeting. For some reason I could not stay in my cell and decided I had to go to this meeting. Even if other inmates saw me go and I would suffer the consequences of their judgement, I knew that I had to go. I didn't care what they would think of me. When I entered the room, I saw two gray-haired guys, Pastor Scott and Brother Walker waiting for the inmates to come in for Bible study. The oldest guy, Pastor Scott, preached of the forgiveness of Christ in the conversion of the Apostle Paul. He explained that Paul was involved with murder, and how he persecuted Christians greatly. Scott showed, through scripture in the testimony of Paul, the simple Gospel, which is the power of God unto salvation. These words touched me greatly and at that moment I felt as if God was doing heart surgery on my heart. After the Pastor finished his message, he gave an invitation to receive Jesus Christ as the Lord and Savior. I was unable to resist. I had been a rebel towards God and engulfed in sin, but at that moment I surrendered my life wholly to Jesus, the Savior of the world. Right away, I knew that I had been set free or at least I felt I had been. Words can't do justice to what God did in my heart. This was so shocking for me. The freedom from a deep bondage amazed me. I went back to my unit, unable to withhold what had happened to me. I started telling my bunkie Tyon what I encountered and from there we beat down for hours. From that day on Tyon and I made a pact to be spiritual brothers. We began reading the bible daily. See Tyon had a similar life as me, growing up Folk, he had reached his breaking point in life too.

I had found my answer as to why I was put back in this institution. All of these experiences I had gone through from college, prison, fame, family and back to my present state were put into place for me to learn, grow and inspire others. As I write these words, I pray not only to get my book and story into every jail and prison in the United States but I want to impact as many lives as I can. Jesus ordered us in Mark 16:15–16 to go into the world and preach the Gospel. My only way to teach others about the lessons I have learned is by telling my story. It is not the story of any saint, but the story of an ever evolving man that wants to change.

# CHAPTER 8

I realize that all that I gained in the streets was not worth all that I lost. Becoming who I am was not worth all of the losses I have experienced. I paid a great expense to become who I am today. One of the greatest challenges I am faced with today is trying to purify my heart. To be honest, all my life I looked at spiritual people as passive, submissive pushovers. However, what I am learning now is that it's actually the complete opposite of passivity. As a matter of fact, in the past when I heard stories of great Christian leaders such as Martin Luther King Jr. and their focus on peace and humility, it seemed weak in my eyes. On the other hand, what I am learning now is that it takes guts, and discipline. My faith is really the only thing that gets me through the days and nights in prison, not even my wife and kids. Honestly, I spend time trying to avoid thinking of them while I'm locked up. Sometimes, I do not even want to call home.

The streets are deceptive because it makes you think you have power, but in reality, at any moment, one wrong decision can take all of your power away. Look at what the streets have given me, lots of pain, death, sorrow, depression, anger, desperation, intoxication and my current state of incarceration. If I could give you my weekly schedule of my life in the streets it would go as follows:

**Monday**-He hugs me and says he is loyal to me.

**Tuesday**-She in some six inch heels smelling good talkin' about give me just one night.

**Wednesday**-They buying me bottles of liquor and pills.

**Thursday**-She is like I like you for you.

**Friday**-He like bro, I would never cross you!

**Saturday**-I'm feeling myself, what more can a NIGGA ask for?!

**Sunday**-God told me on several occasions, get 'em all away son. I have saved you enough, what more can I do to show you the light? You do not want me to remove my hand!

Monday-I thought I was on top of the world, but I was ignorant. My spirit was broken into tears because of my interactions with darkness and I would begin to apologize for my sins again.

This has been a very humbling experience that has taught me so much. It has been so difficult to be positive when my flesh has been filled with rage and revenge all of my life. My life has been nothing but events that have tested me and I have fought so hard to maintain a power that has never brought me any real contentment. However, as I sit here in solace, I'm learning that the real power comes from above and as I am surrendering myself, I can finally just let go and trust that everything will be alright as long as I put my trust in Him.

Behind these walls, I decided to have my first real heart to heart with this so called amazing God I heard so much about. I got on my knees and spoke softly, just barely forming the words on my lips. I felt self conscious and I'm willing to admit it. I started my conversation, "Hello that should be enough I imagine you know who I am, but I will introduce myself anyway, it just seems like the thing to do. My name is Jiwe. I mean Dashaun. Please excuse me, my name is Dashaun Morris and I guess I should refer to you as God or maybe Jesus I heard people call you that before. Or Lord? I understand you go by several titles. I can't recall ever actually praying to you with a pure heart. Anyway, I would like to meet with you today and discuss my life and what possible role you might wish to play in it and thank you in advance for your time and attention." I pulled away for a while not sure what to say next. I figured I'd gotten this far assuming I secured God's attention so I proceeded with my next thoughts. "I'm sure you're wondering what happened and why I took so long to find you. Well honesty I don't think I was ready to live righteous and give up the many pleasures I indulged in regularly. So I figured I could avoid you which would avoid accountability. I guess this is all water under the bridge now?" I started to think to myself, could God actually hear me? I could sense it, I just felt it. It was strange and it was something new.

The feeling made me lose my train of thought, but I began again, "Since you're listening to me, I want to thank you for that. Anyways, I guess I was an angry young boy that grew up Anyway, I decided that I could take care of myself and that's basically the way it went for most of my life. I'm sure you know the story, I gang banged, did all kinds of wild stuff, filled my day with lots of alcohol and drugs and that left me feeling empty and made my life meaningless. I thought it was helping but just pushed my wife further away. Anyways, you know all about that. Okay Dashaun, now where do you go from here, you might as well get to the point. Anyway, I guess what I'm trying to say is that I have moral problems. I've been reading the bible since coming here and it's a good book. It's a fine piece of work and I've come to see that you are a God that values absolute morals. I guess that's what holy means. Actually

I'm glad for that because then we can know where our boundaries are. We could know where we stand. I'm beating around the bush I know."

I gathered my thoughts again and focused on what I wanted to achieve from this conversation. How should I say it? Just what was it I wanted from god? "I guess I need to ask you about your love. I do know it's there. My mother always talks about it and so did Neina and then I had a brief glimpse of it when I talked with Pastor Leaphart. I need to know that you will…" At that moment, I had to stop. Tears were in the corners of my eyes. I wiped them away and took some deep breaths. I began again, "Excuse me. This is difficult. There's a lot of years involved and a great deal of emotions. I was trying to say that I would like very much for you to accept me." I stopped and let the tightness in my throat ease along with the heavy wave of emotion begging to get out. "I've been told that you love me and that you've arranged for all my wrongs, my moral trespasses, to be paid for and forgiven. I've come to understand that Jesus died to pay my penalty and to satisfy your holy justice. I appreciate that and thank you for that kind of love. I want to enter into that kind of relationship with you. I have wronged you and I have ignored you and I have tried to play God myself. As strange as that may sound to you, I have to admit that I have served other spirits during the height of my power on the streets. I led so many astray." The tears were coming again. "Oh well, considering the subject matter I figured what better time to do what I had been suppressing for two decades. But if you will have me, if you will accept me, I will be more than willing to hand over to you all that I am, and all that I have, whatever it may be worth."

I couldn't stop the emotions. My face felt flushed and for some reason I was afraid to go on. But I did go on even as my voice broke, as tears ran down my cheeks and as my body began to shake. "Jesus, I want you. I need you. I need you to forgive me please." The deepest cries of my heart became a fountain, and the Lord and I began to talk about everything. As I poured all of my sorrows and deepest secrets, time just slipped by and the world around me became unimportant. Eventually, I felt like things were different. The man that walked in here May 12th was not the same man today. I now had even more purpose and meaning and felt as if there was still so much potential that was yet to be discovered. Before I had been oppressed and filled with guilt. After this surrendering, I was finally free because I felt that I was forgiven. Before, I was alone and now I had a friend closer than any other.

I'm trying my best to describe this emotion that consumed me, but words cannot accurately capture this experience. I could not believe that He forgave me despite me not having anything to offer him. All I had was me and he accepted me. I was surprised, relieved and finally came to the realization that I did not have to pretend to be Jiwe, Machete or anyone else for him to accept me. All HE wanted was me despite all of my flaws. A load was lifted from my heart and for the first time the darkness diminished and I saw light. I was able to raise my head and for the first time in my life I felt free. Unwilling to let go of this newfound freedom, I wanted to continue to get to know this God who had given me a new meaning to life even though we just met. With nowhere to go and plenty of time on my hands I decided to start from the beginning of the holy bible and understand myself through his eyes.

## Neina's Story

Ever since I was in second grade I knew that I wanted to be a teacher. I was always a nurturer and enjoyed helping others. I went to Delaware State University and majored in Primary Education. I always loved the thought of running a classroom and molding the minds of young children. One thing I always did since I was in high school is have a plan for my life. I learned how important having a plan was from watching my parents and seeing how they were just living day by day. I didn't want that. I wanted a family I wanted structure. Television shows that depicted successful families with love and support showcased all of the things I wish I had. Every goal that I aspired to achieve happened the way I wanted it to the T. My plans were to graduate from high school and attend Del State. It was the only school I applied to because that's all I had my mind set on. Of course I was accepted. When I started school I wanted to be involved in things before the semester even started. I joined the band as a flag girl, eventually becoming captain. My sophomore year I wanted to become a member of the best sorority in the entire world, Delta Sigma Theta Sorority Inc. I crossed over into Delta world April 30, 2002 a day and experience I will never forget. So far everything is on track according to the life plan I had written out.

The last thing to do is graduate, seemed simple to me. I just had one more year and I would be done! Next would be get a husband, have kids and continue to grow in my career as a teacher. Interestingly enough, God had another plan for me, he sent me on a different path the night of February 22, 2003. Little did I know that night at the fight party I would meet my future husband and father to my children. That's the night that my plan would come to a pause in order for me to go through some challenges to make me a stronger woman. It would allow me to really test how hard I could love someone. Here I was this goal oriented, independent and driven young girl. I was on a successful path and my future was bright. Loving Dashaun has thrown several curveballs in my plans.

We were doing well. He finally was putting his family before everyone else. Just like that, he ends up back in jail. I never felt so much weight on my shoulders. Here I am with four children, two dogs, and two jobs. How the hell can I do this? Once again the streets took him away from me. I went through so many emotions from anger to sadness, then feeling pitiful, then becoming overwhelmed and the worst thought was thinking that I was a failure. I felt so many emotions all at once because it was as if my world was crumbling down. All of these emotions going on inside but I still have to put on the face that everything is still normal and daddy is just in New Jersey working. Meanwhile I know that he is really right up the street at Clayton County Jail and there is no telling when we will see him again.

I hate having to lie like this. Our kids have been crying because they have been wanting to talk to daddy. Maybe I can carry this story on for one week, but one month then two months, then the questions are bound to come. At some point they are going to say, "Mommy, daddy never been at work this long when is he coming back?" How am I going to handle the tougher questions and get through this time if they are already getting upset and I am not even sure as to when he is getting out?

My son is at the age where he needs his father because he is in a house full of girls. I am working all of the time I just feel like I am a chicken with my head cut off. Currently, I am trying to maintain bills, trying to fight his case with him and get everything in order to get him home in time for the kid's birthdays. Not to mention the tons and tons of text, inboxes, and general concern from fans and supporters asking me where is Jiwe. Everything that could have gone wrong happened while he has been gone.

Moosey got attacked by a dog, I got into a car accident, and I am falling so behind in bills I feel like I am just going in circles. In addition to all of this there are also the kids' extra-curricular activities. Let's not talk about the intensity of Dashana's track schedule.

I remember the day I told Dashana where her dad really was like it was yesterday. She saw the police in the house, and then she didn't see her dad any more. One thing about Dashana is that she is way ahead of her time. You can catch yourself in a conversation with her and it is as if she was an adult. I talked to my mother in law first to make sure she was in agreement with me about telling her. She totally agreed, if Dashana found out that I kept that from her she would resent me for it. I brought her to my room and let her know that I had something serious to tell her. I wanted to let her know I knew she was very intelligent. I said Dashana your daddy is not in NJ working he is in jail. She instantly busted out crying as if she knew but just had that little bit of hope that it wasn't true. I calmed her down and once she could talk she asked what he did. Not wanting to get into any details I explain to her I'm waiting for details from daddy's lawyer. But in the meantime, daddy has to stay there until this all gets resolved. But he is working on himself while he is in there. I told her to look at it like this. Remember how daddy used to be so angry punching walls and breaking things or would just cry out of nowhere. Well he is getting help to control that. I said you like when daddy is fun and joking around right? Wouldn't it be a lot better around the house if he was like that all the time and not us being worried about making him mad and seeing him explode?

She smiled and said yes. I said ok well look at this as a good thing. Right now he is taking the time to get himself together to be a fun daddy more often. That helped her deal with it. However, every time we would pass Clayton County Jail, I noticed she would intentionally turn her head the opposite way so that she wouldn't have to see the jail. That tore me apart. We don't realize how much of an effect we have on our children. Even though we tried to look at the positive side of it, I knew it still bothered her to the point she couldn't face it.

Track is something special between Dashana and Dashaun. How can I fill those shoes? How can I push her like he did? How can I invest the time like he did? I couldn't, and she is paying for it now. She had almost a year off with a horrible diet and now she is suffering the consequences for it. I feel horrible, but I am doing the best I possibly can by myself. Where the hell are all these brothers he had? The guys who paraded him around all their events for protection. All the guys who would wake him out of his sleep to assist them in all of their bullshit. Where are all the guys that my damn babies called uncle. I never liked this. One thing I have learned dealing with a powerful man in a gang, the friends they have today oftentimes become their enemies tomorrow. I was always mindful of all these guys around my house. I do remember his cousin JP, Junior, and

Jay being the most consistent. Always trying to help, calling me, whatever I needed. As time goes on I am growing a sort of understanding of why God allowed this to happen. Each time I speak to Dashaun, I can tell he is changing. The conversations are not your usual jail talk. His voice is literally different. I am able to notice a change in the way he looks at things and by his explanation of the events he tells me he has experienced spiritually. I can't believe it. Is it too good to be true? God are you finally answering my prayers? I was so excited and nervous at the same time. I didn't want to get my hopes up and be let down when he came home. It's like when do you know to let go and finally accept your blessings. How do you know it's sincere? Faith is the only way to go. That is what has kept you sticking around this long, so why not have faith that this man has finally arrived.

I just continued to pray that this person will stay. This is the man I always knew was in there. The man I so desperately wanted in my life.

He worshiped the ground I walked on. He made me feel so important and so worthy. I finally felt the way I felt when we first met. He made me feel beautiful again. It had been 12 years since he had made me feel this way. I am so grateful that God blessed him and in return blessed me for my persistence and patience. Just another confirmation of how good things actually do come to those who wait.

Although I was always sticking to a plan and I was thrown off course, as an adult I honestly understand the meaning of the saying you don't always understand why God allows things to happen in your life, but it always works out good in the end. It was hard for me to adjust to this idea at first, but I am learning how strong I am even in times of adversity. I see all of the things Dashaun and I have been through, when Dashaun truly found and accepted God into his life I found the man God always showed me he could be. God is so good to us. Dashaun is such a loving and caring person, but he just has so much hurt and anger that it has overpowered his good heart. I am just glad God showed that to me early on in our relationship. If I can pass anything on to any woman out there that may be in a relationship where they know there is better in their spouse, really listen to God. He may be molding and preparing you for something great. Don't give up on someone you truly love that aspires to be better. They may just need love and support to become a better person. I promise God will lead your heart in the right direction. Stay encouraged.

My life without Dashaun would not make me the Neina I am today. I have learned so much from him. I really believe that my life would be an ordinary square life. I would have been your normal 9-5 mom/teacher who is naive to the issues in the world. He has helped develop me into a strong woman that can handle any situation thrown at her. I would not choose a different path for my life to have taken. Now I just have so many good things to look forward to in my marriage.

Now our hard work and sacrifice to keep our family will finally pay off.

I have one final goal I am determined to reach. That goal or vision is to be in my 90's sitting on my front porch in a rocking chair, watching our children, grandchildren, and great grandchildren after our routine Sunday dinner at our house with my best friend, my husband, Dashaun Morris by my side. I can't wait for that day. It will come and when it does I will refer back to this book and just give God all the glory.

---

# CHAPTER 9

***Journal Entry Date: June 30, 2014 Clayton County Jail***

I just finished reading some more of the daily bread and I feel really good. I never knew it could be this exciting. I've learned so much it amazes me and all I want to do is just keep reading till I fall asleep. I'm gaining strength in my darkness. I no longer question why this happened. God knew exactly what he was doing. I feel more strength now. I just decided on Sundays I'm fasting because that day belongs to God. I promise I am feeling something I've never felt before, thank you Father.

***Journal Entry Date: July 2, 2014 Clayton County Jail***

My family came to visit me today. I closed my eyes as I held my babies close and tight. I began remembering all of the turmoil in my life of trying to balance my loyalty to the streets while trying to still be a good father. However, those two worlds constantly competed against one another for importance. In the midst of that, my family has suffered through so much pain, misery and grief. I have been the cause of their sadness for to long. It has been a long road from there to my current state of mind with my babies. In my new future with Neen, the future looks so bright that tears began to fall down my eyes. My oldest asked, "Are you sad daddy?" I held her a little tighter, glancing pass her siblings and her mother who were all smiling with misty eyes as well. I replied in a whisper, "No, I'm just overwhelmed that God finally saved me baby." I kissed her cheek and continued, "I love you my princess, with all my heart." Throughout the years, I always thought the love for my homees and the G-code was extremely important, but seeing my family and their unfailing devotion and belief in me is overwhelming.

It is now 8:30 p.m. and I'm just doing some thinking about who I am and what I've been through all these years and how I got that way. I see why it's imperative we teach our children to stay away from bad things and bad people. It's even more important that we build them a strong foundation so they can create a solid identity. See that is where I came up short. I grew up as a child without an identity. I was a chameleon because of always having to readjust and reestablish myself in order to fit in. By the time I was 15 I had attended five different schools, lived in 4 different states and within these cities live in countless different apartments, so I never got to be comfortable or had a stable situation. This affected me in several ways. My decision to join a gang, invest in a value system that was not defined by spirituality, uphold relationships that were not benefiting me and putting myself in situations that led me to my downfall are all a result of the instability of my foundation. Now when I look at my adult life, I can see the wear and tear it has had on me both emotionally and physically.

***Journal Entry Date: July 3rd, 2014 Clayton County Jail***

It's around 1:30 a.m. and I'm immersed in thought. My mind continues to focus on the flesh. Oftentimes I just want to tell Neen to leave me and let me go so she can live her life and forget me. I sometimes ponder cutting off all communication to allow myself to undergo more suffering. Part of me feels that I deserve torture, part of me still hates myself and what I've become. I know this is my flesh talking. Although I know I can't feel this way, but the flesh does. I have been feeling emotional all day and I fight it with prayer. I try to convince myself that God allows this to happen to bring me to him and will bring me through this so I can continue to find myself living in the spirit, thinking in the spirit, speaking in the spirit and even crying in the spirit. I'm working really hard to avoid the flesh because then I'll be following all these negative feelings.

***Journal Entry Date: July 4, 2014 Clayton County Jail***

Psalm 88 is another favorite scripture of mine. The scripture is a solemn one that speaks of darkness and it begs for God. Being in this prison, I feel the darkness of my life and how all of my actions have led me here. I too am seeking God in this bleak place. I pray that I do not ruin this time and use it to the best of my ability so that when I get back to my family I will be a better person. Once I get bailed out, God will see in the physical how determined I am, although HE already knows because every night I lie on my bunk and constantly replay the choices I've made. I decipher each situation to examine what I would do differently. I'm learning that God has a plan for me. I've heard this for many years, just didn't know what it was.

I believe when we perish, we go before God to give an account. I believe my new life will make the cut and hope that one day I can look him in the eyes, give him a hug and laugh out loud.

Giving my life to God is the best decision I've ever made. I think it's the comfort in knowing this powerful spirit loves me and just wants me to honor him and I will receive heaven. It seems like a pretty fair exchange to me.

I go to court July 20th and then wait for the New Jersey charges, but I know God has me covered. Whatever could have been there to hurt me has already been handled. I just have to walk the rest of this journey and then spend the rest of my life serving. However, I know this time in solitude is necessary for my growth. I'm using this time to strengthen. So far, a lot of progress has been made. My talks with Neen really boost my spirits. The talks help a lot so I just want to get to New Jersey and get out so I can continue this journey. This will be my first time without a squad, crew, or hood backing me. I will just be Dashaun. I am curious to know how I will be. God finally removed all the pieces out of my life to get my full attention. I have so many mixed emotions about life that it brings tears to my eyes. I want my babies to be proud of daddy. I love them so much. Words are hard to find to describe what I feel for Dashana, Dasharie, Dashani, and Lil Dashaun. I am so moved by what I'm learning in here. I learned that God has not left me in my darkness. I learned that this is just cloudy skies that I'm navigating through.

***Journal Entry Date: July 9, 2014 Clayton County Jail***

Success, fame, fortune, glitz, glam, and lights often times only reveal one side of the coin. But my concern lies in what's hidden or in my case there were things I never knew. I thought I had finally figured it out. I definitely had understood and decided that what was holding me back was my affiliation with certain people. I started removing them out of my life and immediately I noticed the blessings and the downside. Doors began flying open, opportunity after opportunity presented themselves, however so did the hate, jealousy and enemies. But what I failed to realize was that I was relying on myself to remove these people and myself to get these opportunities and not God. I wasn't praying and fasting or going to church or reading the word. So how did all the opportunities plus with the lack of spirituality equal success, peace and love? The answer is that it doesn't. I learned that nothing will be blessed if not given from God himself. If he is not the center of your being, ideas, thoughts, and decisions, then you have no foundation and anything you do will not be long-lasting. It's weird to me that the journey I've been on allowed me to see many different things from the top in many cities and in my travels to other countries. But also know that it is not one's riches or success that determines if we are blessed. There are many evil people in this world that have an abundance of physical success, but they lack goodness. In the word, it mentions that the most abundant accomplishment is being able to attain heaven.

I just want my daily bread. I spent so much time focusing on getting rich that I lost sight of who I wanted to really be as a man. I remember how hundreds and hundreds of people contacted me telling me how I had been an inspiration to them. I would do tons of online and radio interviews and I would never give any glory to God. I would never give the credit to him for empowering me with the gifts to motivate and inspire people the way I had been doing. When I think about it, parts of me would be afraid to say it because I didn't want to be seen as corny or uncool or I was embarrassed or not man enough to publicly say I give the glory to God.

At age 33, I now understand the importance of this type of humility and respect towards the Lord. The glory was never intended for us. It all goes up to the Father, and HE will continually pour down blessings. As I am writing this in my jail cell it just sent shockwaves through my body. Let me take a quick break and knock these push-ups out and pray...... (20 minutes later) Okay I'm back after praying and now my pen bleeds. So now I fully understand why we give the glory back to the Father and it's exactly what I do daily. I'm thankful for everything I have. All my talents and gifts are a reflection of the Lord who strengthens me. Some examples are when I refrain from cursing and smile, when I pray for my enemies I smile, when someone does something to provoke my anger, in my mind I just pray for them and take a deep breath. I spend a significant part of my day trying to keep a smile on my face. I spent over two decades wearing a mask drenched in anger and carrying a constant smile is difficult but I'm doing well. People used to always tell me I don't smile enough, but what they couldn't understand was that it wasn't that I didn't want to smile but I was covered in so much sins on top of sin on top of lies and deceit that the devil had a strong hold on me and this prevented me from displaying happiness. Since accepting Christ, putting on a smile has become a part of my daily routine. I see the benefits. Even when I'm alone because of the grace from the blessings helps my head hang high and I have a smile on my face.

When I was reading Matthew Mark Luke, I was blown away by Matthew because of how much of what went on could be many of our current, past, or future situations when it comes to friends, loyalty and deceit. People like Judas are everywhere. These stories in the Bible play a huge purpose in my life today because it shows me there's nothing new under the sun and that if Jesus could be crossed then what should I expect. I found comfort in reading about the deception Jesus experienced. As strange as that sounds, reading about it made me feel closer to Jesus because we shared similar situations of being disowned by friends and I know this feeling. At night, I lay in my bunk in the early morning hours with little light, just enough so that I can fully concentrate on the words I read. I feel myself gaining new life. Sometimes feelings come over me that I haven't figured out how to describe. I call Neen and mom on three-way once a day and that 15 minute call only consists of me highlighting for them all the wonderful things happening to me, inside a jail cell. I can tell that they are proud of me because I hear it in their voices.

Since my bunkmate left a few days ago I have been left in solitude. Some part of me feels it is God who wants this because out of all two floors filled with cells, each one has two inmates per cell. I'm the only cell with one person in it. Since his departure, I have been glued to the word for eight and nine hours a day if not more. I pray 3 times a day where I prostrate. I've taken a liking to reading the daily bread too. I love how personal stories are intertwined with scripture to deliver powerful messages. It is very difficult for me to wait each day to read, I normally just binge read. The Bible provides basic instructions on how to live before leaving Earth. It also is amazing how many times we have to physically be sat down in order to hear God. Take away all the worldly things and just listen. As I read, I listen closely.

My faith is tested daily. Constantly bad thoughts creep in my mind and begin to fill it with worry and anger. Immediately I go to my Bible and begin reading. I do not want my faith to be called into question. I see how Jesus didn't like when his disciples servants would lack faith. So I diligently practice it. While I prostrate, I pray for increasing faith. Revenge on those who got me into all of this mess seeps into my mind. But then I'm humble like Luke 6:27-36 when I read that I got chills. You mean to tell me I have to be kind to these scumbags? But then I thought and read more. If I were to be judged by my sins what names could I be called. And at that very moment I began writing down all the names of my enemies on a piece of paper and prayed for them. I wrote their names, put my right hand over the paper, closed my eyes and let my spirit talk. The things I said were not of my doing, I could feel something more meaningful was behind it. Once I opened my eyes and began writing what you're reading, my eyes began tearing. With the Bible in my left hand and pain in my right I kept writing while simultaneously reading the scripture over and over and over. I read it so much and many tears fell in unison. So much came over me that I dropped my pen, raised both hands and repeated, "Oh father show me your way. I'm nothing please show me." In all honesty these tears didn't feel like tears of sorrow or sadness, ironically they felt like tears of relief! I knew at that moment I have to forgive them. I knew no matter what I would continue to add them to my prayers as I pray for myself. This was not easy for me but for the Lord I would not complain or gripe.

I will begin to impart these teaching into my babies. I have to train them up so they enter the kingdom one day. Their generation is lost out there. I think about how the way we are being raised is the total opposite of the word. We are not taught to forgive, we are taught to get even. We are not trained to be kind to those who slander us, we instead learn to approach them about the matter. I have spent a good portion of my life on the wrong side of the tracks. It is very difficult to break those chains but if we work hard to see God for who he is and his purpose, it is possible to go from hating your neighbor today to loving him tomorrow.

***Journal Entry Date: July 12, 2014 Clayton County Jail***

When you're on top everybody wants a piece. My entourage was able to travel with me, be treated as V.I.P's at clubs, they had access to women, and I even allowed many of them to live with me when they were homeless. I even gave up my oldest daughter's room so that one of them could have more privacy. Neen never complained, but deep down I knew she was tired. If I do the math, within 6 years I let eleven different homees live in my house and I never considered her feelings about this because in my mind a homee in need means say no more. However, down the line when I hit some tough times, they all scattered like roaches. I couldn't understand when I looked to my left and to my right, my closest "friends" were nowhere around. That's when I began to reevaluate my bond with them. I had been used and taken advantage of and even sitting in this cell as I write these words is due to an old friend hating me, then got his baby mama pushing all these shooting charges on me. However, I know there's much good that comes from this experience.

I have a solid blue print to give to my son about male camaraderie, loyalty and trust. I've learned through getting burned to not put more than just a little trust in man for he will let you down but instead put all trust in God. My life experiences will allow me to share my wisdom with my children because I know that the foundation I can provide them with will be something that no college class can replace. I have made several mistakes and bad choices in my life, but my heart has always been genuine and compassionate and my darkest hour got revealed to me when I was looking at my circumstances. My relationships were being looked at in the flesh, when I should have been looking at them spiritually. Today I am thankful for all the toxic people removed out of my life. Yes I'm sitting for now, but what my enemies who basked in my unfortunate situation fail to realize is that they were used as a tool to get me in here in order for me to get closer to God. Even in the midst of their wicked ways, they served as a blessing to me. It has taken me quite some time to come to this understanding.

They have no clue as to how difficult it is to get to this point where I pray for them. I feel as if I grow wiser each day because I continue to digest all of the lessons the good book provides and it continues to help me gain knowledge and understanding of things I was once oblivious towards. There's something amazing to be said about journeys. You never know how they will end, but if you are mindful enough to smell the roses and thorns and continue doing the right thing no matter how it ends you will become more appreciative. Being completely honest, some days I want to lash out like Job. I feel the game cheated me because I didn't get out what I put in, but then again there's no honor or respect in the streets so forget it. The streets wack anyway! I just offer prayer asking for an increase in faith like Job.

I've actually heard most pastors preach the book of Job as a rationale for why bad things happen to good people. I have read the book of Job many times and can't find any proof to support this theory. I believe that the lesson of job is that pain suffering and faith all combined to become the necessary crucible that transform a life from an ordinary one to an extraordinary one faith gives us the assurance that pain has a purpose in our lives we just don't know why it is yet what's unique about job was not his intense suffering but rather his response to it he accepted it with grace and humility one time even thinking God for it.

***Journal Entry Date: July 13, 2014 Clayton County Jail***

For some reason I thought it was the $15^{th}$. When you are locked up you kind of tend to lose track of the days. Sometimes I feel like my life has been through more than enough. I understand we go through hardships to grow but sometimes why can't we just grow without the pain. I'm so tired and exhausted from always having to be strong. To be quite honest, I'm tired of always being looked too for leadership as well. Sometimes, people do not understand the burden that comes along with being a leader. Don't get me wrong, I understand that my life has been blessed because I was given a platform to inspire others and create change.

I remember one of my many blessings was meeting the Dalai Lama. Around this time is when I really started believing I was special. I mean I had been doing things, seeing things, and accomplishing things that no one I knew was doing. Coming from my background, I wasn't supposed to do any of what I was privileged enough to be a part of. In all honesty, to be real with you, I didn't even know the magnitude of who the Dalai Lama was until after our event. We were both at a summit as invited speakers to represent as leaders of peace. Imagine me, a person that society deems as a gangster, a villain, a criminal and a life with bleak outcomes in the same room with a world renowned man who symbolizes peace. Our common thread was our leadership role. At that time, I don't think I even appreciated the impact I had. Often times, we do not take time to recognize our own achievements. I have done that too many times in my life but not anymore now I take each moment in for what it is and enjoy life as I have never enjoyed it before.

When I saw how people were so inspired and in awe of his presence I knew I had to learn more about who he was so that I could understand why they revered him. The first thing I remember doing when I got home was jumping on the computer to Google and research him and was blown away that I had actually gotten one on one time with him. From what I recall, he is a very old man. His security was on everything but luckily I was actually able to shake hands, and after our panel, he offered me great advice. He spoke with a poise and confidence I had never seen before. I was thoroughly humbled at the amount of universal knowledge he knew. I told him about the work I was attempting on the streets and he listened very intently. Afterwards he said leaders are rare. Most people have followings because they are popular or maintain something that others want but there are only a few actual leaders and if I wanted to be one I had to win the hearts and minds of my people. As I was in Mexico at this peace conference with the one of the greatest examples of peace in our lifetime, he gave me a jewel of a lesson that I will remember forever. The greatest thing he told me was that a great leader can start a war at a strike of a match. As he continued the most profound part of this dialogue was at the end of his statement where he continued to say, "But, a powerful leader can end a war, it is easier to start a war or a fight."

I knew it was more important for me to be a powerful leader than just a great leader. Y'all can just go load your guns up, and go look for your enemies. Then, after that they are going to retaliate and now you have a fight on your hands. It doesn't take a rocket scientist to figure that out. However, I know how difficult it is to talk one of your angry warriors out of retaliating or killing. Being a leader from a young age without a strong sense of identity has led me to make poor choices as well. People do not always understand the heavy burden that is placed on your shoulders when your followers look to you for guidance. The fact that one of your decisions can lead someone that looks to you for leadership to their demise is a huge weight to carry.

Carrying this level of responsibility places a toll on you. I just want a shot at being me which I believe is a regular a dad, a husband, and a son. The life I want to live is a life that involves no orders to dish out, no violations, no meetings, no protocols, just me and my love ones. What people fail to realize is one can only be so strong for so long. It's like hanging on a pull-up bar, it doesn't matter how strong you are because eventually hanging on long enough will create pain and you will have no other choice but to let go. I've been holding on to that bar for so many years I feel my fingers are slipping and my grip is loosening. At this point I'm ready to let go not by choice but the pain is too great. I chose to leave my sinful ways in the past. While I was out partying, getting drunk, buying bottles at the strip club, traveling and entertaining groupies to put my homees on, it all seemed good. It seemed like I was doing right. Here I am a black guy that comes from nothing and ends up gaining a lot so I thought I would bring all my friends along for the ride, but actually what I did was increase all my sinful behavior.

So where I used to only drink 40 ounces and Mad Dog 20/20 now I was buying $220 bottles at the clubs. We had two little guns in the hood, I bought 5 bigger handguns and 2 pumps for my hood. Before, I attracted local eights, but now that I was a national gangster sex symbol I was getting pressed by A list models and the finest women around. Despite all of the worldly things I gained, I hadn't actually done anything meaningful. Interestingly enough, as soon as I decided to make changes in my life such as getting away from people inside my camp that I knew would be my downfall, things began to change. Before I knew it I realized that I needed to get myself away from everyone that didn't serve a meaningful purpose in my life. Once I did this, slander, gossip and jealousy came with it. It is just crazy how blind I was to my situation. I couldn't see clear because I was clouded by fame and power. I found life through death and I have found peace through pain. My tears pour like rain when I am alone in my cell. During these moments, I drown out the yells of other inmates, the turning of keys clanking, toilets flushing and the banging of cell walls. All I hear is a still small voice penetrating the darkness of my soul and saying I'll wash you and make you whiter than snow. HE moves people in and out of your life. Some come in to set you back, which ends up opening the door to meet a new person brought in to encourage you to move forward.

***Journal Entry Date: July 14, 2014 Clayton County Jail***

You have more time to sit, be still and listen to him in here. This time is invaluable. I would not be able to go through these changes in the free world because I was driven by money, fame and power. I've been stripped of all those worldly possessions and am down to my bare essentials. The only possessions within prison are my Bible, my life, bread, and water. I see so clear how I allowed myself to be ensnared by the devil's traps. Women, jewelry, money, clubs, and power were all very enticing and addictive. I didn't believe in Him because I was too busy being blinded by phony friends and seductive women. I was so worried about my image and my reputation that I sunk my soul deeper and deeper. I finally understand what it means to sell your soul. I can honestly say I played for the Devil's team. See a lot of my devilish work was masked in films about unity, togetherness, and change, but in my heart I was still sinning daily. I realize that I want to be different. We get out of life what we put in and what I want is total freedom, the kind that man can't take from me.

***Journal Entry Date: July 15, 2014 Clayton County Jail***

I realize what the fight is all about. It's a battle within my body between my spirit as it is in conflict with my flesh to take control of my soul. We have to get in tune with our Spirit so we are no longer overtaken by the distractions of the enemy because the real us is in the spirit and the flesh is just a suit. I have now learned what it really means when people say the truth will set you free. I found the truth. I feel God waited for me in here. He couldn't get to me out there. There were far too many distractions and for this reason alone, my spirit tells me I'm not ready to leave until God finishes what he started. If I allow this process to work naturally and not fight it I will receive the benefits of His grace. Coming to terms with this isn't easy. I missed three of my babies' birthdays.

However, I am staying focused and not letting my sadness overcome me.

***Journal Entry Date: July 17, 2014 Clayton County Jail***

Today has been a so-so day. I haven't called home in a couple of days, kind of just feel out of it. Every day I wake up, I have to remind myself that this was supposed to happen because it is very easy to get down on yourself, let the anger take over and then allow the devil to lead. That's my daily challenge in here. I don't believe in coincidences there was a plan for each of us, a force that brings us together, then twist and binds us into a single length of rope attached to our shared destiny. You were meant to read these words. My family is out there without me, so I pray faithfully that my lord keeps them covered. Some days I want to sleep until this is all over but then it would defeat the purpose. I have to go through these growing pains. There's a plan behind all this so I try my best not to interfere with the process.

As I've been writing this book inside cell 413, I always mail letters home. I'm waiting for New Jersey to come and get me and don't want to run the risk of my notes being taken or misplaced or even taken from me so eventually once I get home Neen will have all of my letters for me in order for it to be transcribed into my computer. I realize living a life without God is like building a house without a foundation. There's no longevity in it. I used to be one of those people that I wouldn't say looked down on spiritual people but I just had this preconception that their lives were boring. I felt like they couldn't do this and do that or can't watch this or can't watch that, they can't party here, can't can't can't. I looked at Christians as people that just couldn't do anything. They couldn't and wouldn't even fight if they had to because they had to turn the other cheek. This was a life I considered lame. Also I've come to realize there's nothing corny about praying or being kind even when people are mean and giving to those who wouldn't give to you.

I also realize how sick my generation is when we celebrate having national crime rates. I remember in 2013, Newark ranked number one as the most unfriendly city in the world. You should have seen the social media posts of some of my old friends and associates. They acted as if having high murder rates and mean people is a badge of honor. This is the devil's work. I never looked at it this way before. How can one celebrate a statistic that reveals a high number of murder victims? Sin is very deceiving because it appears tasteful and smells nice and it may come in a pair of six inch heels with long hair or come in a record deal that promises an abundance of wealth, jewelry, cars, and girls, but controls the content of your music that promotes violence, and murder.

***Journal Entry Date: July 19, 2014 Clayton County Jail***

It all makes sense to me now as to why all of my efforts to enlighten those around me usually came up short. I was not spiritually centered and for several years, I tried to be a guiding force for my peers. Throughout my life, I tried to encourage others and pushed them for change. My hope was that my success would motivate them for greater things. Despite all that I hoped to do in order to instill goodness towards the people around me, I never acknowledged God's role in my success. I now have come to see why so many celebrities waste millions of dollars on cars, jewelry and houses and eventually go broke or become addicted to drugs. Although money may feed immediate hunger for physical satisfaction, the void within our souls can only be fulfilled by spirituality.

***Journal Entry Date: July 24, 2014 Clayton County Jail***

I know what it is to be in need and I know what it is to have plenty. I have learned the secret of being content in any and every situation, whether I am well fed or hungry, whether living in plenty or in need, whether locked up or free. It's having a spiritual foundation.

***Journal Entry Date: July 26, 2014 Clayton County Jail***

One of my biggest challenges was that I felt great anger towards other people and constantly blamed others for my predicament. I realize that I was actually brought into this prison to preserve my life. The lessons I have learned during these past months have given me several tools for survival.

***Journal Entry Date: August 1, 2014 Clayton County Jail***

My probation officer came to see me today. She terminated the rest of my probation in Georgia so now I just have to deal with Jersey.

It literally took me thirty three years to find myself. My life has been full of turmoil. My journey has been rough and painful. I truly appreciate all of you that have been supporters and fans of me throughout the years. I pray I inspire you, but I hope my words ignite you to look into your own lives and put the pieces together in your puzzle of life through seeking God.

It was none other than God that took me from the evil streets of Newark, New Jersey and brought me to the light. My flesh still pumps anger, bitterness, and aggression for those who caused me pain, but my spirit! Listen to me people the spirit in me is what's guiding me. It's my GPS to survive in this world. Since I chose not to retaliate towards my enemies only confirms to me that there's a higher power out there and once we align ourselves with it you can overcome anything.

The betrayals opened my eyes to understanding how the world really is and I've come to grips with who I am. What did I expect? I can't really be mad. It's what the streets have been offering for years. Yes I'm angry, but I'm desperately trying to channel the anger. I fight with myself constantly. God intervened at a crucial time.

***Journal Entry Date: August 12, 2014 Clayton County Jail***

It is 7 p.m. and I realized I was a part of the problem. I look at all the people close to me that took advantage and used me, and I have come to realize as strange as it may sound I wanted to be used. I became dependent upon others to need me. That's how I became so powerful. The go to man was Jiwe. He can fix your problems. Even when people didn't come, if I got wind of the issue, I came to the rescue. I have gotten so used to others needing me that I became hooked. I was taking care of everybody in my entourage. Like the story of Daniel with King Neb, God also took people away from me, my treasures, and my power to humble me. I learned even more once I lost much of what empowered me. It doesn't take a genius to realize it was fool's gold. It wasn't real power. The power I had was just influence that was fueled by my greed for power, money, and fame.

***Journal Entry Date: September 28, 2014 Clayton County Jail***

The G-code will have you 55 years old still shooting fades and 60 years old still attending hood meetings. How foolish.

For so long it's been hard to breathe, focus and relax. At moments I have wanted to toss in the towel and send the guys who turned their back on me and put me in here on a first class trip to hell. Accepting the slander, the back biting, and lies forced me to dig deep within for Christ like strength. I mean for grown men to run around creating lie after lie wanting credit for things they were not owed was crazy to me. It's like they emailed, texted, face booked, tweeted, and instagrammed everybody that would listen just in order to talk bad about me. The funny thing is that my reputation speaks for itself. Those that believe this craziness are those that are easily influenced by gossip. I am learning a lot in my trials as I await the outcome of this case. I learned patience and the importance of picking my battles.

The thing is before I was trying to save everybody. See when you come from the bottom like I did with a group of people who all have nothing and you begin to get a little something like a little success or are all of a sudden looked at as a celebrity, then you feel burdened with the responsibility of making sure they are also happy. I felt like I owed everybody and I felt guilty about having more than my brothers so I was over compensating by splurging on them and partying with them just to balance it all out. I felt obligated to shower them with materials, travel, exposure, in order to internally feel like I was worthy of the opportunities I was getting.

Coming here has given me the time I was not afforded in the free world to sit and be still while receiving spiritual food. I understand now that God will strip you of the distractions of the world to sit you down and get your undivided attention. With no other books to read on this tier and no bunkee for two weeks I was able to gain control over my mind and completely submerge into the scriptures.

***Journal Entry Date: November 1, 2014 Essex County Jail, NJ***

I was moved from Clayton County jail and extradited to Newark, NJ to answer to the charges that were pending out of East Orange. This process requires approval by the state governor. You can imagine my concern for the outcome of these charges especially due to the severity and detailed caution that was taken to process my transport. Let me explain to you what a flight extradition is, basically you are shackled from hands to ankles in cuffs, put on an airplane and in my case, marched through Atlanta airport for all to see. I dreaded this process. Just two months prior, my movie Deathcoast had just premiered in the theaters so my name was buzzing heavy around the country. I was one of the newest filmmakers who made that hot movie about Newark, New Jersey.

However, here I am being escorted through

Atlanta airport with two U.S. Marshals. I was so humiliated. I saw person after person that knew me or recognized me.

I had been through an extradition process before, but it did not involve this level of humiliation and the fact that I had more exposure because of the recent film release made it even more difficult to walk through the airport with my head held high. By the time I arrived to Newark airport, it was apparent that even more people recognized me and I felt ashamed. All I felt was the piercing stares. People were not seeing the young man who had so much promise, to everyone that saw me that day, I was just a criminal.

This has been such a long road. I was looking at myself in the mirror tonight and I really keyed in on my face, chest and neck. I was trying to see if I could see beneath all the ink. As the time passes by and I am trying to see my true self, I found it difficult to see my real self. Tears welled up in my eyes while I stared at the stranger before me. Who are you? I felt a huge wave of emotions rush over me like a violent current. What have you done to yourself? I just knew there had to be something deeply hidden in this man who stares back at me but what? All my life I had the great ability to break someone's personality and traits down in a matter of moments but here I am before myself with 33 years worth of insight and I have not got the slightest idea.

***Journal Entry Date: November 21, 2014 Newark, NJ***

I have been sitting in the county in New Jersey for almost a month and I have been trying to post a $350,000 bail. The Prosecutor was playing hard ball and requested a source hearing. Basically, they want to know where the funds and property are coming from in order to finance my bail. Neina gathered up the money and a list of co-signers. I am very fortunate to be friends with Glenn from right away bails in Hillside. He allowed me to post the bail for 1%.

While I been here in the county, I was housed with my co-defendant G'Mack. Yea, you read it right, the charges I'm facing I also have a co-defendant who was given the same charges. Soon as I arrived on the tier, he spotted me from his cell. As I enter my cell, I have a bunkie, so immediately I run through my checklist. I do a quick once over of his body checking for tats, I scan the cell for writings on the wall, anything to help me see is this a enemy or potential ok bunkie. Nothing sounds my alarm. G'Mack has been here the past 6 months so it was good to see my dawg again. We develop our routine talking and working out every day. Most of our day involves strategizing about how we can prove our innocence in this case. My family was able to post bail and the C/O just came in to tell me to pack up. As I exited the tier, I slide a kite off to G'Mack with some parting words. As soon as I am outside, I took a deep breath of air and thanked God for opening those gates. Now, I have the opportunity to prove that I can be the man HE wants me to be and I have to use my freedom wisely in order to ensure that I can remain with my family and no longer have this case over my head.

# CHAPTER 10

I am home with my family and I am so excited about being able to finally be the man they deserve to have in their lives. One of the first orders of business is to look for employment. Let's see, so I have never had a real job before. I mean considering the life I led, working a 9-5 didn't fit into my lifestyle. Besides, I never really saw the need to work a steady job since I had other means to make money. I have contributed to supporting myself and my family through various speaking engagements around the country. The career as a motivational speaker has been good to me and I have been speaking since around the world since 2008. I began making $500 an event to now making $2000 per event. This worked for me because I was never the clock in and out type, so in one hour I was making what most made in a month. In my mind, I figured as long as I had at least two speaking events a month I was straight. However, there's no consistency in it and there were up and down months. Sometimes you would do three or four speeches in a month but, then you would go months without anything.

Before back when I was still running the streets money flowed to me by other means, less legit ones, but once again I never had no 9-5, I had no one to answer to, I would watch others doing that daily grind working for the man and I'd just sit back thinking to myself that ain't never going to be me. Contrary to my earlier beliefs about working, somewhere along the way, life begins to change how you view things. I now realize the risk of getting fast money is not as appealing as getting safe money without that risk. The fast street money was good except with that came the possible consequences of things like being locked up or shot, always having to look over your shoulder to make sure no one caught you slipping. With a legitimate job those aren't things you worry about. I do want a life where my money comes through legal means and since speaking engagements can only cover so much then that means I would have to find another way. It is necessary for me to find a legal one that brings in some extra bread but doesn't put me or my family at risk.

Now here I am attempting to fill out a job application online. I definitely wasn't comfortable with this position. I can only imagine how much more uncomfortable it must have been back in the day when you had to get all dressed up in your Sunday best, go into the place of business and ask for a paper application that in most cases you filled out right there on the spot and handed back to them. That was back in the days when if the manager on duty didn't like the way you looked your application went straight into the trashcan. At least on the internet, you don't have that worry about that, at least not until you get the interview. I stare at the screen in front of me as I read the questions. I'm a fairly intelligent guy, yet some of the questions I have to admit that I'm not even sure why they are asking me. I get frustrated easily by stuff like this. Makes it easy to see why young guns stay on the street, hell it's easier than trying to go legit in some cases.

Have you ever been convicted of a felony? Now I have two felonies that would make getting a job difficult. Damn this question, I have always heard it holds so much weight, it wipes your chances out completely. I don't know what to check, Yes or No. I talk with a few people and I get mixed answers. Some say be honest and tell them and later make them understand. Others say lie, hopefully they don't check. So I'm all confused. After talking to mama, she advises me to be upfront, and in the interview explain the charges to them. So I receive an email back for this forklift job. I was so excited they emailed me back. A date was scheduled and I was ready to get this job. Now here is my dilemma. My face tats. What the hell are they gonna' think of what I look like. Damn, all my years in the street I never considered how my face would be the determining factor of whether or not I will be hired by a job. The way my life was in the past, I just never thought it was going to be an issue, hell I was never going to work for the man right so why even worry. So much of my past continues to make my present more difficult. I made several of these decisions when I could only see one future not realizing all of the other possibilities that were still available to me.

Too many times people dig themselves into situations and get mad when the world responds not to their liking. I ain't blaming the man who is reading the application for seeing a felony listed and not giving me a chance or the woman who goes to interview me and sees the tats and thinks this is not the image we want for our company. Some people see beyond these things and are willing to say "hey I'm going to give you a chance" many do not. As much as you might want to lay blame on them for that, you can't because at the end of the day you were the one who made those decisions to commit the felonies or get the tats and in doing so you made the decision to allow them to judge you for that when they are deciding to hire you or not. As much as you may want everyone to be forgiving of your past and accept that you are in a better place now then you were in the past, some people just won't see your progress. They don't have time to see it or a desire to. All you can do is keep moving forward and making the changes in life that you know are needed.

It's definitely an adjustment going from controlling the minds of killers, the slickest guys on the planet to being given instruction from a guy who could have been no more than my water boy on my high school football team. This is definitely a humbling experience. I find it very funny to see how power can shift quickly. I went from being a powerful man on the street that controlled the lives of people to now going into the work world and now having to adjust the power that I once dished out to now respecting the power of another man that I could merely crush with a text message. I guess this is really just a matter of transitioning myself out of a mindset that was used to earning respect through violence and my status and instead utilizing my credentials and experience to earn respect from people. It's very humbling to now have to interact with coworkers, many of whom have never been through the slightest bit of difficulties that I have faced so they really never understand me. I mean at the job they really don't get me because I'm very quiet and I'm not very social, so it is very difficult for me to interact with them but I try to put a smile on my face and not offend anyone. However, I did get pretty cool with two guys, Javonte a local from Georgia and Nayquan a Jersey native from Trenton. They have both informed me how my silence and face tats make some of my co-workers uncomfortable. So I am mindful of attempting to be a little more inviting and social.

It's all a process. Most of my life, I've dealt with nothing but gang members and now I'm dealing with normal civilians. It is funny sometimes thinking of me with a job that has benefits such as paid vacations and a 401k. I mean how did I go from the Bighouse to the Warehouse.

Too many of those running the street aren't even thinking about the future consequences of what they are doing, or that one day if they are going to ever step away from that kind of life what will they need in order to make this kind of transition. I was able to make it to college but couldn't make the transition. I couldn't keep the worlds divided, for some reason back then I could not walk away from a life that was destroying the other one, keeping me from attaining my full potential. I was fortunate enough to realize the path I was going down and was able to correct that before it cost me more than it already had, but far too many don't realize this until it is too late. They lose their family, freedom and their life before they are able to get things in order. Many cases, a father figure is what they crave because in too many cases the fathers aren't around. The person the kids are looking up to has to be someone with a strong character and is teaching them to do the right things not how to rob a liquor store without getting caught, and not how to sell drugs on the high school campus without getting busted. If we are going to properly prepare our children to go out into the world and be productive members of society it takes a village.

We are losing every day in the streets. Sometimes we are too closed minded to see the bigger picture. When you look at the amount of us that are incarcerated you have to see that there is some sort of connection between the prison system and all the availability of ways plastered before us in our communities that make it so easy for us to be sent there. I look at how many years mama struggled by working 2 jobs and never having more than a couple hours a day to actually see me and my brothers. There were times I'd go days without seein' mama. Also I played sports. Every time I walked outta' my house, I always saw dealers chasing down car sales. I observed them counting money and because of the struggles my family was facing, I was envious that we didn't have money like these dealers. "How can people like this have so much money doing practically nothing while mama is catching 2 buses in the winter to get a check from 2 jobs at weeks end that still couldn't accommodate all our bills let alone any extra money for myself and brother to buy things young boys need."

I couldn't understand this. I had never cared about drugs because I knew first-hand what it did. I watched mama OD twice. Both times were as a child. I was 12 and 13 when I saw this. I had an immediate dislike for that white powdered substance. Here are these older guys that sold it so freely while wearing nice clothes, nice sneakers, and cool winter coats. Inside I was angry. Over time, the wear and tear from month after month of struggling to be able to squeeze $10 outta' mama just to attend the school dance my anger changed to desperation and I said screw this. I decided to talk to one of the neighborhood older guys and he got me my first pack and immediately I understood and saw the benefits in drug dealing.

The streets are not safe and they do not offer you shelter or love. All they have to offer you is the question of what have you done for me lately. The lifestyle will demand that you do more, become things that you never wanted or thought you could or would become to satisfy the hunger that is now feeding on you.

One of my goals is to keep this kind of thing from drawing kids into the mix. It's tough because parents have to be increasingly vigilant as their kids are growing up. Don't let people like I was back in the day around your kids, but that's hard to do when you working two and sometimes three jobs at a time just to pay the rent and keep the lights on. It is not an easy world we live in and when you come from a home where there isn't a lot of money it's even harder because not only are you worrying about where your next meal is going to come from but as a kid growing up you see all these things that your friends have and you want them too. Are they necessary for life no but are they things that make you accepted by your peers so hell yeah you want them.

Gangs in and of themselves are not a bad thing not in their origin anyways. They started out as a way for kids without a lot of support in the home to have a place to hang to make sure they were taking care of each other. That is a good thing, but once the criminal element took hold like anything that is once good it became tainted. Sure the kids are learning, granted they learning the wrong things but they getting an education. It's one about violence, deceit, how to do things that don't benefit anyone but themselves or their set. They are not learning skills that will help set them up in a position to have a job where they don't have to worry about someone walking up and shooting them because they are in the wrong hood. The question is how do we get all these kids to make the transition from gang banger to becoming a productive citizen. It's not an easy answer because I know the lure of the streets, the power that it offers and how the street life can intoxicate you. I heard homees tell people "I make more in a day on the corner selling weed then you do all week." It is hard to combat that mentality because simply telling them that yes you do but at least in my job there is no chance I'm going to jail isn't going to sit well with them. Their response is always going to be, "I'm not going to jail. I won't get caught." That's the problem when trying to educate and make changes among a certain mindset. The bad things like being gunned down or locked up "ain't never going to happen to them." We as a society have to break that mentality. We have to offer more then what we are offering and show these kids that there are better ways of living. For me it took almost 20 years of my life and finally being in a cell knowing that everything good and honest that I had worked for might be taken away from me, that my loved ones were getting the raw end of my decisions because daddy wasn't home at night or that Neina was having to raise the kids for a long period of time without me due to decisions I had made.

I have a lot to lose. I have four kids, a loving and wife, a home, and a level of notoriety and even with all that going for me, I still ended up almost losing it all because of my associations and the poor choices I made in my past.

As I sit in my new home, I'm constantly reminded of the life that awaits me. There was nothing in those streets for me except a conviction or casket. One of the hardest things I have ever had to do was make the choice to part ways with the street life. Why you ask? The streets were the fabric of my being. It was everything I was made of from my thought patterns, behaviors, tendencies; they all were rooted & cemented in the bricks. It's funny that when you are young you see life through young lenses. As you grow older so should your perspectives. The one thing I despise about the streets is that the rules and regulations aren't intended for anyone to grow, mature, and move on. Its rules require you to remain ignorant, lazy, destructive and selfish. It is almost to the point that when one has survived the struggle in them and decides to want to make an honest attempt at living a normal life, those same streets will turn on you. The rules are rigged from the beginning.

The man I am today is a man that survived a life style that intended to kill me. A life style designed to have my kids raised without a daddy in the home. I very much love waking up to my baby girls feet and legs all in my face when I want to versus hearing a C/O yelling at me at 4:30 a.m. to wake up and make my bed. I love this life. God has preserved my life to live. I can only hope and pray that many of you that still are slaves to your sinful nature understand quickly that we only get one life, and with that life our outcomes are based on the choices you make. I am no better than the little homee hanging on my old city blocks in Newark & Irvington. My beginnings were exactly the same and in most cases a bit more severe, but it's the resilience in us that separate those that are able to get out and live a decent life compared to those who choose to continue to live a miserable life with no purpose.

I am proud to have used my life as a walking trail of the do's and don'ts. I know my purpose is to inspire a nation one soul at a time. In my heart as you read this, I know there must be an ounce of "I want to live a better life too" in you. We all deserve to have a blessed life. We have to stop seeking instant gratification. It requires heart and guts to fight the fight. It requires discipline to do what's right when everything and everyone around you embraces wrong. So I dare you to be different. I double dare you to go against the grain. I triple dog dare you to make your own path versus following everyone else's. Trust me when I say nothing about my change had been easy. In fact, I still have to be mindful to live in the spirit because my flesh can still become weak and react. If you have an ounce of respect for me, then trust that I'm telling you the benefit of living a god fearing life is priceless.

# CHAPTER 11

Malcolm X is a name that resonates throughout history. He was a man whose actions changed the course of the world. Sometimes I feel as if today's generation fails to realize the real struggles and barriers we must overcome. He fought battles during a time when black people did not have the rights they have today. I have to wonder where both he and Martin Luther King would stand with the recent riots involving police shootings in places like Ferguson or Baltimore. Would Malcom be leading the revolt, while Dr. King tried to calm the masses?

In 2006 I had the opportunity to meet Malcolm X's grandson who went by the name of Little Malcolm. I was introduced to him through Terrie Williams and his aunt Ilyasah Shabazz. He had just come home from jail and I went to New York to meet him. I had known quite a bit about his situation because it was a part of Black history. It was an honor to be meeting Little Malcolm. We hit it off immediately because we were both very knowledgeable about African American history, but I know the real reason I was there to meet him was because his aunt wanted me to focus on his new gang affiliation with the Bloods and through much more research in conversations with Malcolm I found out that him running with the Bloods in jail was his act of rebellion. He felt that the Islamic community pushed him out over the loss of Betty Shabazz and his joining the Bloods was just a way of him wanting to be accepted and that's where our relationship began through countless hours of conversation and countless hours of dialogue. He would come to visit me in Newark and I was going to New York to visit him. I was always very cautious and mindful of the things I said to him considering who his grandfather was but the bottom line of what I was trying to get him to understand was that he came from a legendary family. Things that his grandfather started in this country and the principles that he enforced many of us still live by to this day and when I consider the path that he was on was bringing shame to the family name. I tried to point out how it's hurtful to your loved ones and it does not align you with the tradition of the X family name. From there we began to build a bond to get him back in tune with who he was supposed to be and shortly thereafter Malcolm began traveling more and walking in the footsteps of his grandfather.

I'd like to say he wanted to finish what his grandfather started. This brings me to the situation when Malcolm went to Mexico. I knew he was going and from my understanding it was business so while he was out there I had gotten an email from Little Malcolm and in the email he had asked me could I help him out with some finances. Two days later after the email was sent, I received the tragic news that Little Malcolm was killed in Mexico. I actually read his email the day after and it was very difficult for me to deal with this because I wish I had more time I would have definitely sent that money and it weighs heavy on me that reading the email and sending the money could have been the difference in his life being spared. In addition, a few months prior to his death Malcolm was in my movie Deathcoast Str8 outta Newark and we had a powerful scene. Til' this day I still watch our scene over and over. It's amazing to me how he was speaking life into me. I was asked by his Aunt Ilyasah to speak about Malcolm at the funeral, in which I did. I talked about our friendship and how his flame had been extinguished too soon. As I stared out over the mourners one thought ran through my head, "I have done this too many times in my life, too many that I have known have died, have been lost to violence there has to be another way, a better way."

# CHAPTER 12

During my college days, I remember a psychology professor walked around on a stage while teaching stress management principles to an auditorium filled with students. As she raised a glass of water, everyone expected they'd be asked the typical "glass half empty or glass half full" question. Instead, with a smile on her face, the professor asked, "How heavy is this glass of water I'm holding?" Students shouted out answers ranging from eight ounces to a couple pounds. She replied, "From my perspective, the absolute weight of this glass doesn't matter. It all depends on how long I hold it. If I hold it for a minute or two, it's fairly light. If I hold it for an hour straight, its weight might make my arm ache a little. If I hold it for a day straight, my arm will likely cramp up and feel completely numb and paralyzed, forcing me to drop the glass to the floor. In each case, the weight of the glass doesn't change, but the longer I hold it, the heavier it feels to me." As the class nodded their heads in agreement, she continued, "Your stresses and worries in life are very much like this glass of water. Think about them for a while and nothing happens. Think about them a bit longer and you begin to ache a little. Think about them all day long, and you will feel completely numb and paralyzed – incapable of doing anything else until you drop them."

At the time I understood what she was saying, however the importance of this lesson did not resonate until recently. I have been carrying so much baggage throughout my life that it caused me constant pain and aggravation. It's important to remember to let go of your stresses and worries. I am now learning that no matter what happens during the day, I must let go of the stress that same day and not let it carry into the next day. Once the weight carries into the rest of your days, it is a strong sign that it's time to put that glass of stress and worries down before it overwhelms you. One of my biggest burdens was to remove myself from the people that I thought I had to maintain my loyalty to. In addition, the temptation to go back to the streets is also hard to overcome.

I now understand that there are powers and unseen forces in the darkness of this crazy world that focus on ruining you. They will even risk their freedom and life to end yours. At this point I realize no gun I possess can stop this attack and as soon as I realized this, I know the only way to win is with the protection of God. He is the only one that can save you. So as you are reading this I'm sure many of you that feel this way are asking how do you accomplish and overpower the thoughts, worries, stresses and emotion that overwhelm you throughout your days? My short answer is by understanding and working against the enemy's method of operation.

From my experience, the majority of the evil thrown at us by the enemy is done in the late night hours of midnight to 3 a.m. That is when the enemy's attacks usually come. Many of the tragedies I endured over the course of my life usually occurred between these hours. Either these tragic events occurred during this time period or I received the news of a terrible event in these late hours. I don't know why they choose these hours but from my experience this when all the bad things happen. So if you intend to defend yourself and combat those forces, then you need to be up when your enemies are up. You need to be awake when they are awake; you need to be at work when they are at work. You have to learn the secret of putting your spiritual ammunition to use when the enemy is firing at you. Basically what I'm saying is, if you can understand night time warfare, if you learn the secret of getting up in the midnight hours for spiritual warfare, you stand your best chance at victory. I am a living witness to this. I know what it means to be up at 12 midnight and pray until I'm tired. Each time I carry out this drill, I wake up in the morning and feel spiritually taller, focused and stronger. Why? I was up when my enemies were up. I had my spiritual guns blazing when my enemies were shooting their arrows. Even in physical warfare, in all my years fighting in the streets, 85% of our attacks were carried out at night. We'd get liquored up, pill and drugged up, banging turf music, all just waiting for the sun to fall, night to come, then our playground was set.

We'd wait 'til' midnight, I mean literally that was the standard time, and then we'd attack our enemy's bars, after hours spots, homes, and number blocks while they partied and was content. I have been heavy in my studies blending those teachings with my life experiences and I've come up with the realization that many times the enemy will send surprise attacks against God's people, that's why we hear things like "Oh! I ain't see it coming!" Well how can you see it coming when you sleep? The best time to fight physical and spiritual war is at night. The enemy understands that and the earlier we understand that the better it is for us. I feel that these new generations of people are so weak in sacrifice. It is because all they want is the gain but do not want to suffer no pain. There's a price to pay and one of those prices is getting up at midnight, 1 a.m. or 2 a.m., and walking up and down in the room, around yo' house aggressively praying and taking authority, and control over every power of the enemy working against your life. Trust me, this isn't easy to do consistently. Your flesh will rebel. Just five minutes into your prayer, your flesh will be wanting to tap out and go back to sleep. You have to be stronger and say to your flesh, "My flesh, you are under direct orders to my spirit, those who are fighting me are not sleeping, why should I go to sleep." Then you should continue praying and get ready to silence every outburst of your flesh. You have to disappear somewhere really far in your mind. Before you realize it, the time is already 30mins later or even an hour depending on how severe your attacks are coming.

This is the secret I discovered in order to find strength. I'm cautioning you all because you cannot afford to sleep when your enemies are actively hunting. Wake up at midnight and waste away your tears of frustration your tears of pain, and your tears of revenge to god. See I know how most people's prayers are superficial. They spend no time dedicating their time and effort into showing devotion yet they want everything. They do drive by praying. This is the price many are not willing to pay. It's the most expensive price you will ever have to pay that won't cost you a dime except your time.

Now I told you I have been heavy in my studies and when I look through the Scriptures, I realize that the most violent battles ever fought in the Old Testament went down at night. Here are a couple of my favorite prayers: "In his days Edom revolted from under the hand of Judah, and made a king over themselves." "So Joram went over to Zair, and all the chariots with him: and he rose by night and smote the Edomites which compassed him about, and the captains of the chariots: and the people fled into their tents." (2 Kings 8:20-21)

Joram did not go over to Zair in the morning, afternoon or evening. He went in the middle of the night and defeated the enemy. He was able to succeed because they were sleeping. "And Saul said, Let us go down after the Philistines by night, and spoil them until the morning light, and let us not leave a man of them. And they said, do whatsoever seem good unto thee. Then said the priest, Let us draw near hither unto God." (1 Samuel 14:36)

My emphasis on attacking at night has been revealed in the bible repeatedly. For those who feel vulnerable during these hours, my advice is to seek God and spirituality help you fight temptations. I am baring my deepest truth for every eye that reads my words, there is a real live war going on around us. You need to get off your comfortable bed, get on your knees put your face on the floor, and attack first, disrupt the momentum destroy their strategies before they move on them. There have been plenty of times I'm lying in bed and am jolted up by an evil nightmare of my death, I know now that's god waking me up to pray. People don't ignore that. It's a defensive tool in your favor. You just have to understand its benefit. When that happens, at that very moment I feel there's meetings, text, phone calls going on right at that time and attacks are being deployed against me. Learn the discipline of self-denial. Everybody likes to sleep at night, no one likes to be awake when they should be asleep. After all, we have been busy all day and the night is the best time to rest, but just like Saul said, if we are going to win we have got to go in the night. Therefore, they went in the night to ruin the Philistines until the morning light. This is exactly how spiritual warfare operates in the night. This is the secret of warfare; this is how to weaken the enemy and this is what the devil uses over and over again against us.

Here are some more scriptures that describe these nighttime attacks:

*(Jeremiah 6:5)*
*Arise, and let us go by night, and let us destroy her palaces.*

*The enemy comes to steal, kill and destroy. When? In the middle of the night. In other words, each time night comes; warfare starts in the realm of the spirit.*

*(2 Kings 19:35)*
*And it came to pass that night, that the angel of the LORD went out, and smote in the camp of the Assyrians an hundred fourscore and five thousand: and when they arose early in the morning, behold, they were all dead corpses.*

God used this strategy over and over in the bible. Many of those demonic forces that work against you during sun up are only the hitters that get their orders during sun down. So at this point in my book some of you that are so glued to the streets are probably thinking I'm crazy. Hey I probably would too. It's also most likely because I have an understanding that you don't. So next time god wakes you up in the middle of the night, he didn't do so for you to spark that blunt, twist the cap off the liquor, or to bust your rifle, but instead he may have done it to wake you up and help you save your life.

# CHAPTER 13

I have lost so much time to the prison system; I have lost too many friends to jail cells and short-lived lives. Today is a precious gift and trust me when I say that I am enjoying this new walk of life. Since being home and committing to live my life away from the streets and dedicating it to my family and faith, God is truly blessing me. This past Sunday pastor Leaphart prophesied over me that this week something amazing would happen. Now let me be clear, I was never fond of seeing pastors lay hands on people because I never believed it was real. Well on this Sunday, pastor did just that. See, he is a man I've come to love. I admire his leadership. I admire his marriage to 1st lady. I admire his love for his people. So as he is laying his hands on me as if he was some type of fortune teller, I could feel all kinds of emotions that I still can not explain. During that week it proved to be a good one with me receiving the news I had been praying for.

I have been home for 6 months trying to make sure that I will be around to raise my children. Exactly one year ago, I was swarmed at my house in Atlanta by the FBI and arrested for 3 attempted murder charges, 3 aggravated assault charges and numerous weapons charges that stemmed out of East Orange. I was able to leave Essex County Courthouse and what pastor spoke over my life came to fruition, my case was officially dismissed. Charges dropped! One thing I know when dealing with the legal system is that if you don't have proper representation often times you will lose your freedom. When I began fighting my case I knew that I needed a lawyer that knew his way around the court, so I hired Jonathan Gordon. I just couldn't believe I was going through this again and once again back before a judge. In these types of cases, you feel helpless and it becomes draining to navigate through the justice system without good representation.

Throughout my legal proceedings my

attorney kept me updated on my next court date. I paid this man $10,000 and his job was to protect me. So as we have each court date I was living in Georgia and about once a month I had to fly back to Jersey. After pastor prophesied that a blessing was coming my way during the week, that following day, Monday morning my lawyer called me with the news that the prosecutors offered a deal to drop all the charges if I pled to a petty disorderly charge. I contemplated the idea of it and decided to go with it. I had been fighting this case from the street for six months and it's finally coming to an end. The day that the charge was dismissed was like one of the most refreshing days of my life. I felt a huge burden lifted off my shoulders as I left the courthouse. I've learned so many lessons about betrayal, deceit, envy, jealousy and loyalty. I've even allowed myself to be put in many of these bad predicaments because of my love for people but now as of today I realize that I have to live for a higher purpose. I'm thankful for this experience and in the fact my trust and belief in God has grown because of all of these predicaments. When I was down he was there. I don't want to go celebrate by getting whacked off the liquor. I just want to prostrate and give thanks.

I now can live with peace of mind and have new levels of understanding. My role as a father is not merely a title. I am an active parent and I carry daily responsibilities for my family. My family exemplifies the true definition of what family truly is and this feeling of accomplishment makes it easy for me to brush off the pain from my shoulders from the people who have turned on me despite the many "helping hands" I have extended. Society has conditioned people to move in individualistic manners, however because of the compassionate and giving person I am I have found it often times trying for me to juggle being a "real man" to my family and a "homee" or friend to the streets while simultaneously pursuing a professional career.

Time has afforded me with a deeper wisdom and thus, by escaping the darkness of my past I have been blessed with the gift of light which has restored my vision to see clearly that I cannot have both. Ties needed to be broken especially, if I am going to remain triumphant from my past demons. I cannot be pulled into the "big fish in a little pond" mentality again. My life ahead has greater promise. I have been trapped for too long and have made countless sacrifices staying true to a "code" that cannot guarantee my family the life they truly deserve and, I have made the unwavering decision to choose my family and myself first and I am truly unapologetic about this choice. This is where my true warrior crown resides not in the streets. So yes, I do feel like a "fish out of water" in these new territories of what I could never see in my past peripheral. Living outside of that urban box while maintaining the respect, dignity, and integrity has lent unmatched testimonials to my motivational speaking career;

serving as a guiding force to inspire people from all walks of life across race, sex and class.

This new walk of life that I'm journaling is extremely uncomfortable at times because you take a man like myself and understand my background and understand the things that I have accomplished the places that I have traveled, the people that I've affected and inspired and you will understand that I do serve a purpose greater than what the exterior and my physical may present. I've been the underdog my entire life and at the age of 34 I still feel like the underdog because I'm doing something that has not been done much of in the inner cities. I'm fighting against all odds that are stacked against me. So yes I do feel like a fish out of water and at times it is very difficult to breathe.

I am no longer running from my demons but rather I am running toward greater promises. As I stay on the right side of the road my nightmares are disappearing and my dreams are manifesting into lived experiences of speechless victory. So you see, it has been quite uncomfortable to become a leader of positive success and peaceful truce because my past marked me just another number, another inmate in a cold dark box, I should have been dead but, faith has seen me through it all and faith forever will serve as the true source of my power. I cannot erase what happened in my past but, what I have the power to do from this day forward is to make better decisions not only for myself and family but, also for the daily increasing fans I have so when they see me they see hope. My hope is that they gravitate towards faith instead of fear and the light that I extend by never giving up on myself gives them the strength to shine bright and therefore, they can have the courage to walk away from their darkness too.

Much of my past continues to follow me even as I have embarked on a different way of life. My battle scars are displayed for everyone to see and can cause many to have preconceived notions of the man I am today. However, my story articulates the evolution of a man who learned from the mistakes of his past and is redeeming himself by becoming an exemplary father and mentor to other fatherless young men looking for guidance. My message for everyone is to not judge a book by its cover. Although my allegiance to the Bloods has left a mark on my physical being, my spirit continues to fight the war of cleansing my soul. I end this by telling all those that see my flesh before my spirit, don't let my tears fool you.

*Dear Readers,*

*There are times we all need support and guidance. In my opinion, the best advice comes from those who have lived through obstacles and persevered. Do you have a young son, nephew, little cousin, or little brother ages 9-17 that's out of control? Do you need someone to intervene?*

*I have had several families reach out to me for help in order to overcome situations that seem hopeless at times. In order to provide added services to families in need, I am willing to provide private virtual mentoring through my foundation entitled "Against the Grain." Families can now reach me via skype, email and telephone to schedule personalized consultation services for your loved ones. For more information, please contact me via email at Dontletmytearsfoolyou@gmail.com with Mentoring in the subject line.*

*Sincerely,*

*Dashaun "Jiwe" Morris*

## *Special Thanks*

I gratefully want to acknowledge my team beginning with my creative writing partner Bob Dixon. We've spent many hours emailing, texting, and speaking over the phone in order to work on this project and I am forever grateful for your help, creativity, consistency, and dedication to bringing my story alive.

Next, I have to thank my editor Liza Chowdhury. Your countless efforts last minute to step in and spend dozens and dozens of hours formatting, structuring, and making my story flow was a solid blessing. Considering how demanding I am, you dealt like a pro. We did it!

I must give a huge shout out to my personal assistant Quiana Jameson. I don't think I personally could do for you what you do for me. Especially with how demanding I am. Your ability to multi- task and keep all my business in order is beyond me but nonetheless, I am grateful to you and all that you do for me. You really make my life easier Q. From booking my flights, hotels, researching any and everything I need, to organizing my travel schedule, I can only feel privileged to have you in my life.

To my marketing/publicity team, I thank you for keeping my name buzzing. We set out a goal back in June to cover all grounds, nothing off limits was the motto and we are following through with that. More to come, let's keep climbing.

To all my readers, fans, and supporters, I thank you deeply for allowing my life to steal a few moments of your time. In a world today where most people don't even enjoy reading, you all have demonstrated to me that you cannot hide information from US. Thank you

This book could not have been written without the encouragement and support of my family, wife Neina and kids Dashana, Dasharie, Dashani, and Lil Dashaun, I love you all more than you can imagine. I'm thankful for your patience with all my traveling, and nights I took time off from daddy and husband duties because I was locked into writing this book. I know there were many days & nights daddy was all cranking because I was struggling with my sentences, word play, metaphors, and overall flow of book, and y'all sometimes caught the end of my frustration. But the little hugs from you TyTy & Booty meant something. Moosey you texting me while I'm cooped up in my room to say I Love You Daddy work hard put a smile over the frown I had. Lil Dashaun you always busting in the room trying to do pushups & pull ups in the middle of my thoughts was priceless. And finally Neen, I know you dealt with the most with my being standoffish, quiet, moody, snappy, and tired all the time. You know how I get when I lock in, I obsess so thanks for being patient. With all my time, resources, and energy I exert in inspiring the lost around this country, it is the 5 of you that put me back together when I come home broken and drained. Thank you. Y'all know our saying #ImmediateFamilyOnly #AgainstTheGrain

Last and most certainly not least, I'm down on my knees, prostrating and thanking God. I can never be thankful enough for all of the mercy, grace, and favor you've shown me. I'm not worthy of a fraction of what you have blessed my life with.

## FIVE QUESTIONS WITH DASHAUN

1. **After reading this book, what part of my old lifestyle do you think was the hardest for me to let go of?**
2. **Did you ever struggle with regrets from your past as I did and how did you deal with it?**
3. **What part of the book surprised you the most?**
4. **How can we as a community work together to help kids that may have gone through what I went through from becoming involved so deeply in street life?**
5. **Has the book inspired you and if so how?**

   ***Send all answers to**

   **Dontletmytearsfoolyou@gmail.com**

Bonus footage: https://youtu.be/4Qiz57Ay-Sk

Thank you for reading my story. I would like to hear from you so feel free to hashtag #DontLetMyTearsFoolYou for twitter & instagram, include comments pictures & reviews.

*I didn't write this book for Dollars: I wrote it for Change!*

40135082R00145

Made in the USA
Middletown, DE
04 February 2017